FISHING SKILLS

THE COMPLETE
FLYFISHER

Tony Whieldon

Introductions by Russell Symons

WARD LOCK

Acknowledgments
My thanks to Michael, Graham and Bob, whose
invaluable assistance made the marathon a little
shorter.

A BLANDFORD BOOK

This edition first published in the UK 1993
by Blandford
(a Cassell imprint)
Villiers House
41/47 Strand
LONDON
WC2N 5JE

Distributed in the United States
by Sterling Publishing Co., Inc.
387 Park Avenue South, New York,
NY 10016-8810

Distributed in Australia
by Capricorn Link (Australia) Pty Ltd
P.O. Box 665, Lane Cove, NSW 2066

British Library Cataloguing-in-Publication Data
A catalogue record for this book is available
from the British Library.
ISBN 0-7137-23580

Typeset by Litho Link Ltd, Welshpool, Powys,
Wales

Printed and bound in Finland

Contents

General Introduction

Fly fishing for trout is rightly regarded as one of the most subtle of all angling disciplines, and during the last few decades has experienced a dramatic growth in popularity.

In the 1960s, a Government decree allowed what were then Britain's Water Authorities to make their storage reservoirs available to the public for recreational purposes. Stillwater trout fishing was born, and began its astonishing growth in popularity at that moment. Stillwater fly fishing for trout has become a highly valued hobby, skill, even obsession, to over one million participants. Increasing numbers of sea and coarse anglers are drawn to the reservoirs at the beginning of each season to add fly fishing to their repertoire of fishing skills, and perhaps to enjoy a change from their usual surroundings and sport.

It doesn't matter if you are a complete newcomer to fishing or already an experienced angler from another discipline. If you are to become a successful fly fisherman/woman, then learning to cast a good fly line is the essential skill. A good casting style will enable you to fish with precision, throughout a long day, without your casting arm becoming too tired.

It is all too easy to fall into the trap of spending a lot of money on tackle before learning to cast a good fly line is *the* waste, and can set back your casting ability and hinder, to some extent, your ability to catch fish.

No matter how well intentioned your friend is when he offers to teach you to cast, go to a professional casting school as soon as you can – most certainly before spending hard-earned cash on tackle! Ask the professional's advice, try the different rods, reels and lines he will have available. This is all part of what you are paying the professional to teach you.

Your first rod, reel and line can influence your casting style for life. Once a bad habit is established, it will become a subconcious reflex and, before you know it, you will have a flaw in your technique that can take yards off the distance at which you are able to present a fly – yet all the time you remain blissfully unaware of what has happened.

The price of carbon-fibre rods has tumbled in the past few years and it is now possible to buy an exellent rod at a quite reasonable price. The rod should be over 9 feet (2.7m) in length; surprisingly, it is more difficult to cast well with a short rod than it is with a longer one. So don't buy a shorter rod in the mistaken belief that it will be easier to use. But in any event – and it bears repeating – go to a professional school and get some tuition and unbiased advice.

Fly lines are another of those contentious subjects on which there is always the friendliest of animated argument amongst fly fishers. It will pay you to listen to what the professional has to say, then walk the banks of the fisheries that you intend to fish; watch, look and listen to what the successful anglers on those fisheries can show and tell you. Have a natter with those anglers who are 'resting' but, whatever you do, avoid interrupting someone who may be concentrating on stalking a particular fish. Most anglers are polite and more than willing to chat, but interrupt them at the wrong time and you could well suffer some icily verbal abuse (see the section on bankside etiquette).

It is also a good idea, at this stage, to join a local fly fishing club. This will give you the opportunity to ask for and receive advice on all manner of fishing-related subjects. You will also probably be treated to many entertaining half-truths that have been stretched further than they have any right to be!

Another advantage of joining a club is that during the winter months it will probably run a fly-tying class. Your local adult education centre may also run such classes and it is well worth the effort to attend. Not only will tying your own flies save you money, but the experience of landing a good fish on a fly which you have tied yourself is one of the most satisfying aspects of fly fishing. At first you will probably find yourself tying all sorts of wonderfully fluffy, highly coloured lures, but in time you will graduate from them to the often simple, traditional, easily tied flies which have endured and caught fish for generations of fly fishermen and women.

Make sure, when you step on to the bank for the first time, that your fly box is well stocked with some of the classically simple flies such as the Black and Peacock Spider, Stick Fly, Pheasant Tail nymph and Sedge pupa. Other modern classics such as the Montana, Viva and Appetiser are also well worth their room in your box. These will be sufficient to catch fish under most conditions. Indeed, a few of the very best fly fishermen/women rarely use more than half a dozen patterns right through the season, and catch just as many fish as any of us. A classic example of the rule which applies to all forms of fishing is: 'keep it simple and straightforward'.

When the author, Tony Whieldon, asked me to write the introductions to his book, I was both honoured and a little horrified at the task, because I know him to be a very able fly fisherman. What he has done in this book, as well as to demonstrate his superb draughtsmanship, is to show you his down-to-earth grasp of the information you need to know to catch trout, and I know he will join you with me in wishing you 'Tight Lines'.

Russell Symons,
Plymouth, Devon.

Rods

Modern fly rods are man-
ufactured in glass fibre,
carbon fibre and boron.
Carbon rods are always
recognizable by their slim
butt area just in front of the
handle. The slimness belies
their power for they are quite
capable of throwing a line
40 yds (35m) or more.

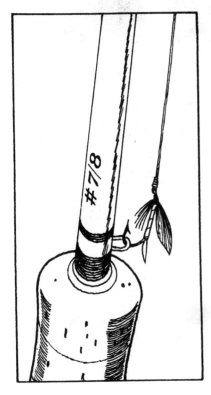

Just above the handle, on
the rod itself, a number will
show the manufacturer's recommended line size for use
with the rod.

In this instance a size 7 or
8 line would be suitable.

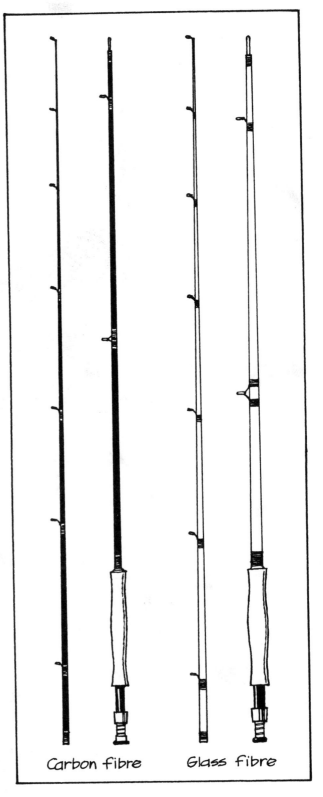

Carbon fibre   Glass fibre

Reels

Single action

SINGLE ACTION

As the original function of the fly reel is to store line in a convenient package, this reel with its uncluttered design is the one used and favoured by the majority of fly fishermen.

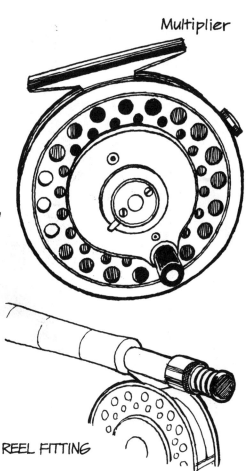

Multiplier

MULTIPLIER

For extra-fast line retrieve this reel excels. If you prefer this design, as many do, frequent lubrication will prolong its efficiency.

Automatic

AUTOMATIC

This reel strips line back onto the spool very fast, with the aid of a spring mechanism. Simply press the lever to keep in touch with a fast moving fish which is heading towards you.

REEL FITTING

It is a matter of choice which way the reel is secured. Some anglers have the handle on the right side, while others prefer a left-handed wind.

LINES

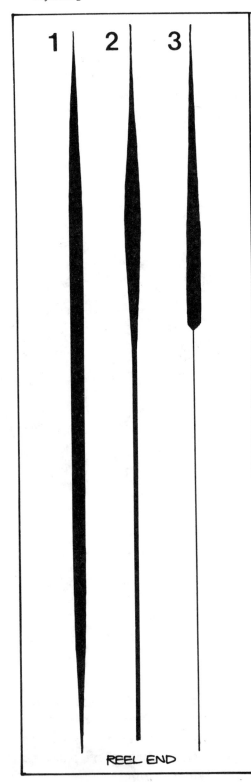

1 DOUBLE TAPER (DT)

The standard length for a full fly line is approximately 30yd (27.43m). The DT is ideal for delicate presentation when fishing at close to medium range, or when loch-style drift fishing from a boat.

2 WEIGHT FORWARD (WF)

Longer casts can be made with this line, but it does have the drawback of creating a disturbance as it hits the water. However, it is a very useful line for general shore fishing.

3 SHOOTING HEAD

This set-up is usually a home made affair comprising 35ft (10.50m) of DT fly line and at least 50yds (45.5m) of braided monofilament or solid monofilament shooting line, plus backing.

Shooting heads are also available from some tackle shops.

REEL END

The profiles shown previously can all be obtained in different densities – here they are.

1 FLOATING (F)
For fishing a dry fly or a wet fly in the upper layers, or a weighted nymph in the lower layers. Some floating lines have a sinking tip (SF).

2 NEUTRAL DENSITY (N)
Extremely slow sinking line with a multitude of uses when the upper layers and shallow water is being fished.

3 MEDIUM SINKING (S)
For searching different depths and fishing a lure or a nymph at mid water.

4 FAST SINKING (S)
For fishing close to the bottom in medium-depth water.

5 ULTRA FAST SINK (UFS)
For fishing close to the bottom in deep water.

6 LEAD CORE
For exceptionally deep work in deep lakes. Especially useful when trailing lures very close to the bottom, from a slow – moving boat.

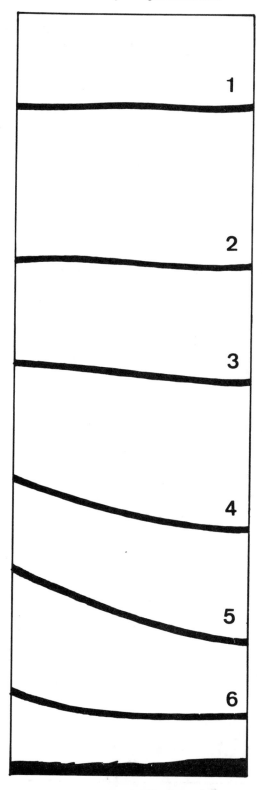

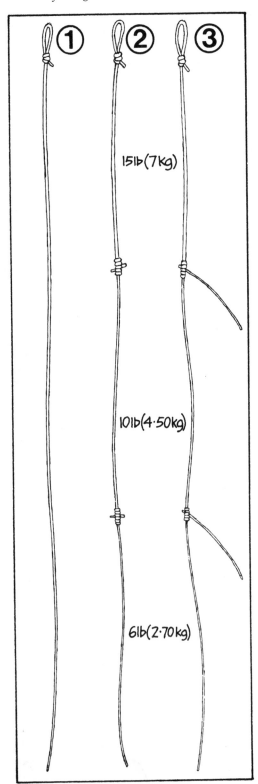

① 15lb(7kg)

① 10lb(4·50kg)

① 6lb(2·70kg)

Leaders

① KNOTLESS TAPER
For fine fly presentation these are the best, but they have one drawback; during the course of use, and after a number of flies have been changed, they obviously become shorter. This means that what started as a leader with, say, a 4lb (1·80kg) point will eventually become a leader with a 5lb (2·25kg) or a 6lb (2·70kg) point.

② KNOTTED TAPER
Many anglers today purchase small spools of nylon of different breaking strains and make their own. All that is then required to maintain the length is a new section of nylon at the point, which is connected to the rest of the leader via a blood knot.

③ TAPERED WITH TWO DROPPERS
This type of leader is mainly used for fishing loch-style from a drifting boat, although there is no reason why it should not be used from the bank.

The breaking strains shown are typical of what may be used when fishing a water where the trout run to around 10lb (4·50 kg) in weight. A finer section of, say, 4lb (1·80kg) may be added if the trout are smaller, or when using very small flies.

Connecting line

It is convenient to have a permanent coupling length of nylon about
24in (60cm) long fastened to the end
of the fly line. When a new leader is
required it is a quick and easy
operation to replace it. The standard
overall length of the leader should
be about the same length as the rod.
If fishing a leaded nymph from a
floating line over deep water, the
leader would obviously have to be
longer.

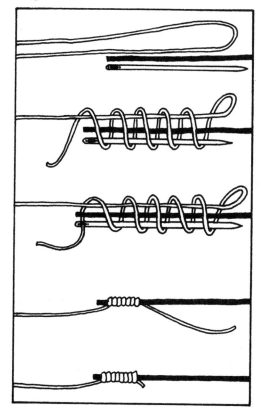

Knot for fastening leader to line
and line to backing.

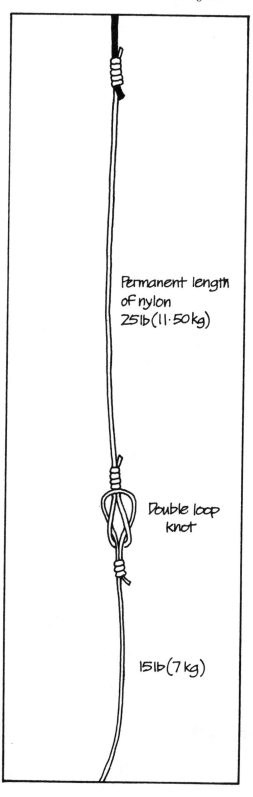

Permanent length
of nylon
25lb (11.50 kg)

Double loop
knot

15lb (7 kg)

LOADING THE REEL

As the overall length of a fly line is no more than 30yd (27m), it is advisable to increase the volume of line on the reel by adding several yards of backing. The amount of backing needed will depend on the size of the reel. To find the answer, wind the fly line on to the spool; attach the backing to the line then wind the backing on to the reel until it lies about ¼ in (6mm) beneath the housing supports. Remove the backing and line from the reel, reverse, and rewind, backing first. Attach the backing to the spool with the knot shown below.

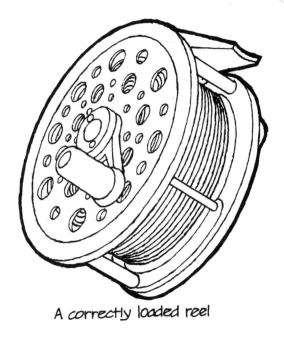

A correctly loaded reel

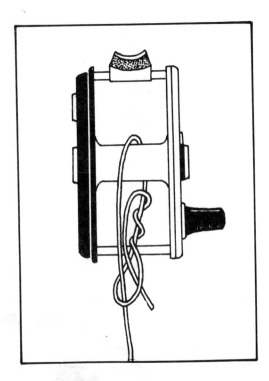

LINE TO LEADER

Needle

Fly line

15lb (7kg) nylon

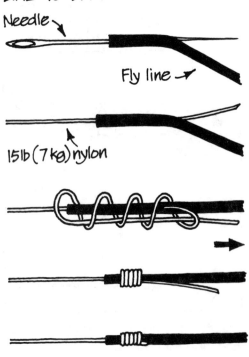

LEADERS (Butt end)

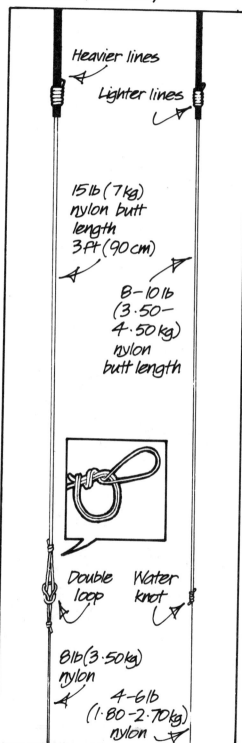

Heavier lines

Lighter lines

15 lb (7 kg) nylon butt length 3 ft (90 cm)

8−10 lb (3·50−4·50 kg) nylon butt length

Double loop

Water knot

8 lb (3·50 kg) nylon

4−6 lb (1·80−2·70 kg) nylon

COMPLETE LEADERS

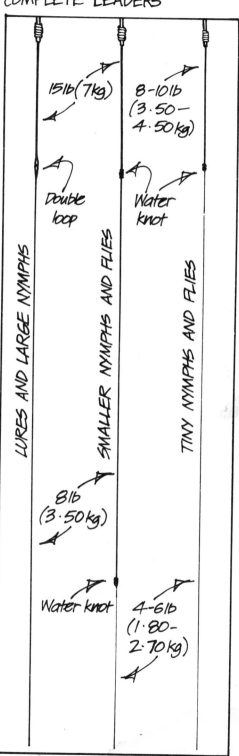

15 lb (7 kg)

8−10 lb (3·50−4·50 kg)

Double loop

Water knot

LURES AND LARGE NYMPHS

SMALLER NYMPHS AND FLIES

TINY NYMPHS AND FLIES

8 lb (3·50 kg)

Water knot

4−6 lb (1·80−2·70 kg)

15

DROPPERS

Droppers can be added to the leader at any time, with a four-turn water knot.

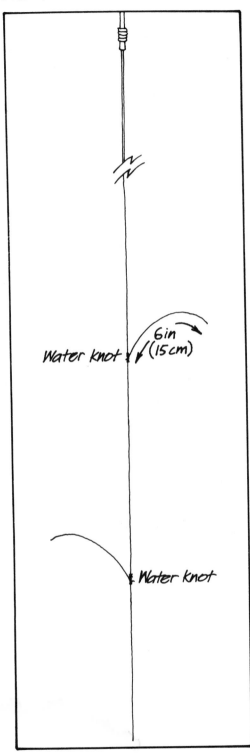

Water knot $\leftarrow$ 6in (15cm)

Water knot

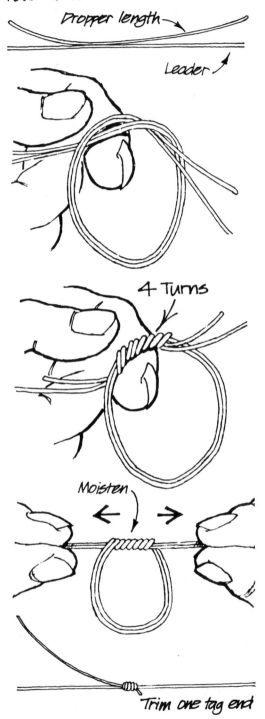

Dropper length

Leader

4 Turns

Moisten

Trim one tag end

CONNECTING A SHOOTING HEAD

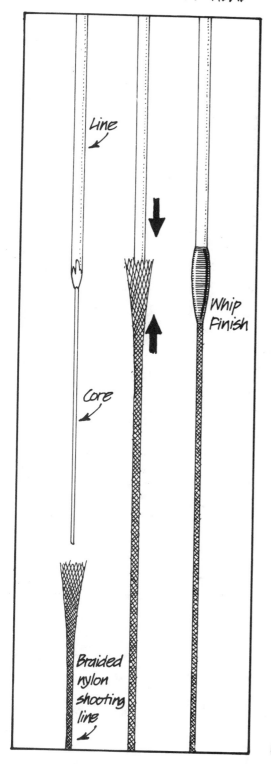

Line

Core

Braided
nylon
shooting
line

Whip
Finish

POWERGUM

The inclusion of this material in a leader permits very fine points to be used even when large trout are present.

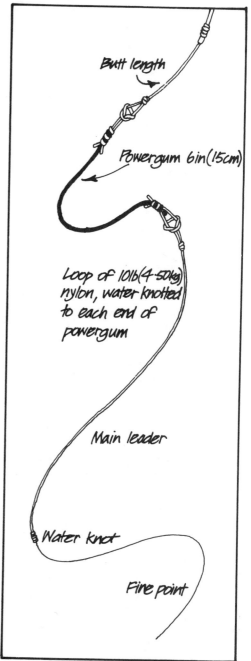

Butt length

Powergum 6in (15cm)

Loop of 10lb (4.50kg) nylon, water knotted to each end of powergum

Main leader

Water knot

Fine point

17

Fly hooks

SPROAT hooks with a turned-down eye are probably the most ideally suited hook for the traditional wet fly patterns.

SPROAT hooks with a turned-up eye are used for dry flies, although some anglers prefer dry flies tied on the down-eyed hook.

Lures, and most nymphs are tied on long shanked hooks with a turned-down eye.

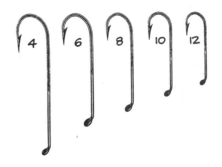

Artificial flies

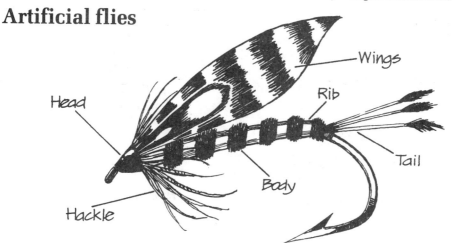

Head

Wings

Rib

Tail

Body

Hackle

DRY FLIES

Used when fish are taking insects from the surface. Equally effective on river and lake. Most dry flies are tied with the purpose of imitating, as closely as possible, a particular species of insect.

WET FLIES

Some of the traditional wet fly patterns bear some resemblance to aquatic life, but on the whole they are bright and flashy. The smaller, hackled wet flies used by the river angler for upstream fishing are, on the other hand, most life-like.

LURES

These probably account for more stillwater trout than all the other types combined, mainly because of their more widespread use. Colours used in their construction are as varied as the spectrum. They represent small fish rather than aquatic insect life.

NYMPHS

Mostly fished in conjunction with a floating line. Some patterns are weighted by the inclusion of lead wire beneath the body material. Of all the artificials, these are the most life-like. Patterns vary from the very small buzzer pupae up to the large damselfly nymphs.

Nymphs

Amber Nymphs

MayFly Nymph

Damselfly Nymph

Pheasant Tail Nymph

Damsel Wiggle Nymph

Stick Fly

Collyer's Nymph

Montana Stone

Persuader

Brown Caddis

Mayflies

These artificials represent the largest of the British mayflies, Ephemera danica, which appears on rivers and lakes during May, June or July.

Fan-winged Mayfly

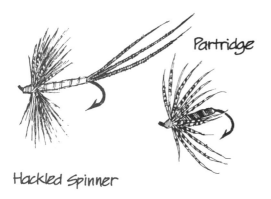

Partridge

Hackled Spinner

Hackle-point Spent Spinner

Popper lure

Anything less like a fly is hard to imagine, but this cork headed creation can be cast well enough with orthodox fly gear, and accounts for many good trout.

Use in conjunction with a floating line and retrieve with long steady pulls, across the water surface.

Casting a fly

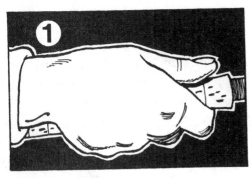

Hold the rod with the thumb on top of the handle....

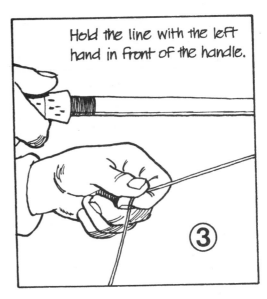

Hold the line with the left hand in front of the handle.

.... then pull enough line from the reel to provide enough weight to get the rod working properly.

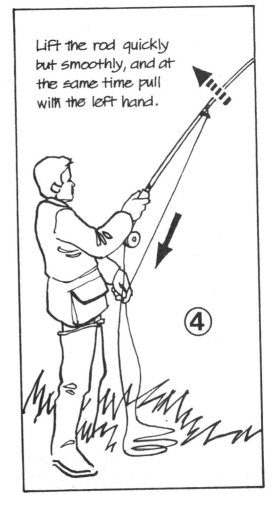

Lift the rod quickly but smoothly, and at the same time pull with the left hand.

Casting a fly

⑤ Stop the rod here. A common fault with many beginners is to let the rod fall back well beyond this point.

Pause in this position and let the line straighten out to the rear. If it helps, watch the line in the air.

⑥

.... and as the line unfurls over the water, release the line from the left hand, the 'shoot'!

⑦ Drive the rod forward....

⑧

Fishing a floating line

When the fish are active up in the surface area, and especially if you can see insects being blown on to the water surface, and being taken by the fish, it is worth using a dry fly.

Before the fly is cast, it should be 'dunked' in a bottle of floatant.

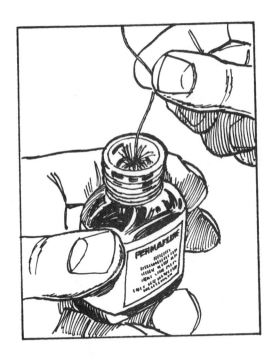

Dragging the fly across the surface in short erratic jerks will often produce a response.

A floating line can also be used to fish a nymph on or very near the bottom. In this case the leader will have to be longer than usual, (15ft (4·55m), and the nymph will need a weighted body (leaded nymph).

Whenever nymphs are being used, it is advisable to give the leader a wipe with 'leader sink'; a good substitute is washing-up liquid.

Fishing a floating line

Sometimes a trout will be seen leaving a trail of rings as it cruises just beneath the surface, sucking down insects which lie in its path. By logical deduction, it is possible to place your offering accurately ahead of the fish.

Next estimated rise

Present fly here

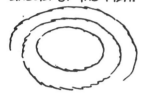

As nymphs or pupae rise to the surface to hatch, they are often intercepted by the fish before they reach the surface. This activity is perceptible only to the keenest eye. Binoculars are a great help when trout are feeding like this.

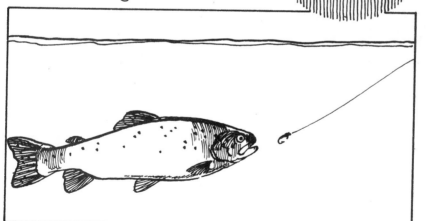

After the cast, pause awhile to let your nymph sink well beneath the surface, then retrieve line very slowly, pausing occasionally to keep the nymph about 12 in (30 cm) under the surface film.

Fishing a sinking line

Of the different types of sinking
line the very slow sinker is the most
versatile. It can be used to over—
come a cross-wind problem, or to
fish a nymph or lure in the upper
layers of water, or over weedbeds
and underwater snags.

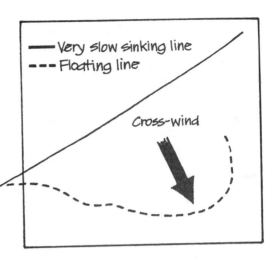

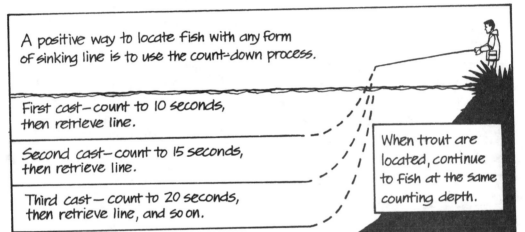

A positive way to locate fish with any form
of sinking line is to use the count-down process.

First cast—count to 10 seconds,
then retrieve line.

Second cast—count to 15 seconds,
then retrieve line.

Third cast—count to 20 seconds,
then retrieve line, and so on.

When trout are
located, continue
to fish at the same
counting depth.

The way to retrieve a lure

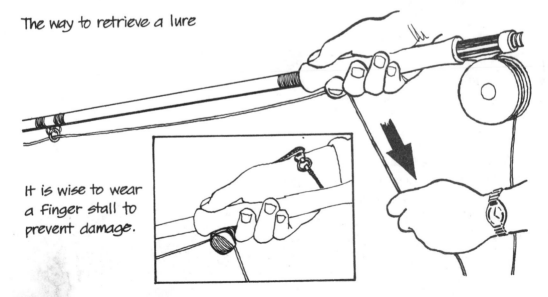

It is wise to wear
a finger stall to
prevent damage.

Fishing a sinking line

Although the very slow-sinking line is versatile it would not be practical to use it exclusively, as it would take far too long to sink to fish that were lying well down in very deep water.

When searching for fish in these deeper places use a fast, or very fast sinking line.

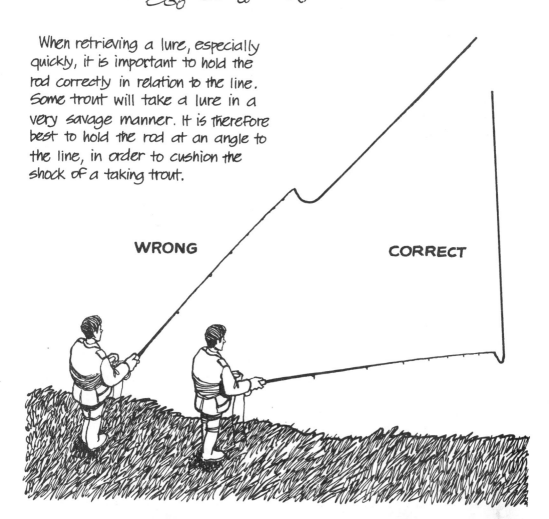

When retrieving a lure, especially quickly, it is important to hold the rod correctly in relation to the line. Some trout will take a lure in a very savage manner. It is therefore best to hold the rod at an angle to the line, in order to cushion the shock of a taking trout.

WRONG

CORRECT

Species

BROWN TROUT (Salmo trutta fario)
  This trout is indigenous to
Great Britain and Europe, and is
found wherever the water has a high
oxygen content, from the acid streams
of high ground to the more alkaline
waters of lower ground. Acid-water
trout seldom grow to any great size,
unless they have an unusually rich
food supply.

RAINBOW TROUT (Salmo gairdneri)
  Introduced to Europe and Britain
in the 1880s, it is used extensively
to stock man-made fisheries, but
does not breed, except in a few
places where the conditions are
exactly suitable. Distinguishable by
the magenta stripe along the flank.

**AMERICAN BROOK TROUT
(Salvelinus fontinalis)**
  This fish is more a char than a
trout but can be cross-bred with
both the brown and the rainbow
trout. A brook/brown trout cross
is known as a 'tiger trout'.

Cannibal trout

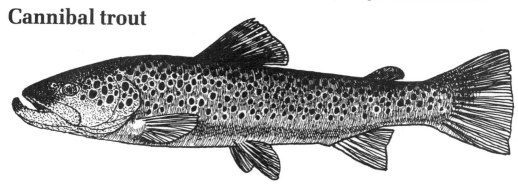

Old male trout very seldom bother to feed on surface-borne insect life, except, perhaps, when a heavy hatch of *Ephemera danica* is taking place.

They adopt, instead, a diet consisting of small coarse fish and trout. The nomenclator is very apt, for they can be as rapacious as any pike.

Ghost Swift

These predatory trout can be caught on lures. The perch-fry streamer is probably the best bet. At dusk and during the night they often swim near the surface, and can be caught on an imitation ghost-swift moth.

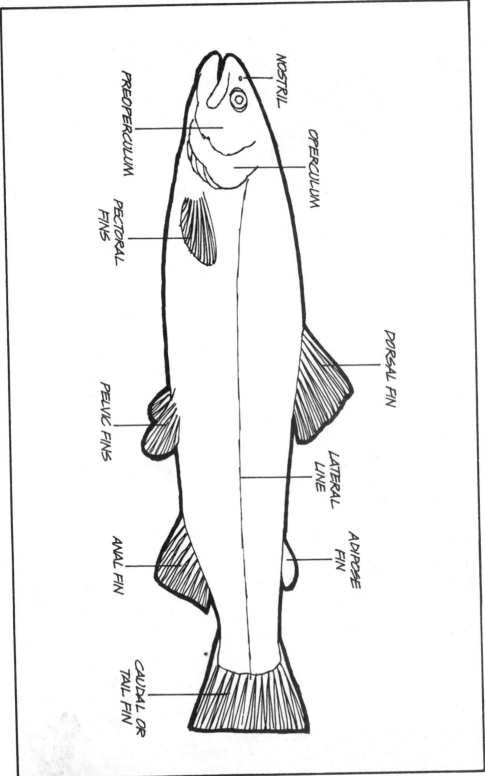

NOSTRIL

PREOPERCULUM

OPERCULUM

PECTORAL
FINS

DORSAL FIN

PELVIC FINS

LATERAL
LINE

ADIPOSE
FIN

ANAL FIN

CAUDAL OR
TAIL FIN

EPHEMEROPTERA (Mayflies)

The trout's diet

Members of this group of insects all have upright wings and two or three long tails. There are four stages in the metamorphosis: egg, nymph, sub-imago and imago. Fishermen refer to the sub-imago as the 'dun', and to the imago as the 'spinner'.

At the surface the 'dun' emerges from the nymphal skin.

The 'spinner' then emerges from the 'dun'.

After mating, the eggs are deposited into the water, and both male and female fall to the water surface as 'spent spinners.'

Nymphs are also taken by trout as they swim towards the surface.

These dead and dying flies are easy prey for trout.

After hatching from the egg the nymph lives and feeds on the bottom. Some are eaten at this stage by foraging trout.

The trout's diet

Other groups of insects go through a similar sort of development as the Ephemeroptera. All the stages shown below form part of the trout's diet.

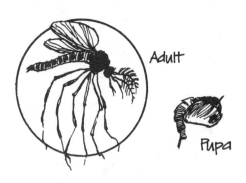
Adult

DIPTERA: In this group, the midges (Chironomids) are of most interest to trout.

Pupa   Larva   Larva (bloodworm)

TRICHOPTERA: This group includes the caddis or sedge flies.

Caddis larvae in cases

Pupa

Adult

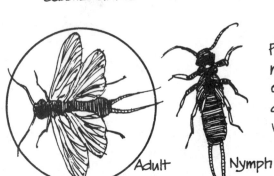
Adult   Nymph

PLECOPTERA: These are found mainly in stony rivers. The nymph of the large adult stonefly is very active, and is a main food item where it occurs.

ZYGOPTERA: Adult damselflies are occasionally taken by trout, but the nymph is a main food item.

Nymph

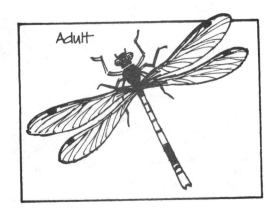
Adult

The trout's diet

Many other species of non-aquatic insects form part of the trout's diet. These are blown on to the surface of the water by the wind. Here are the two most commonly encountered.

Hawthorn fly (artificial).

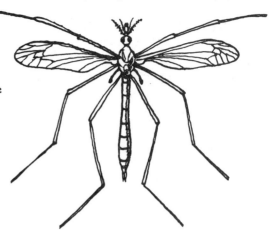

Crane-fly or 'daddy-long-legs'.

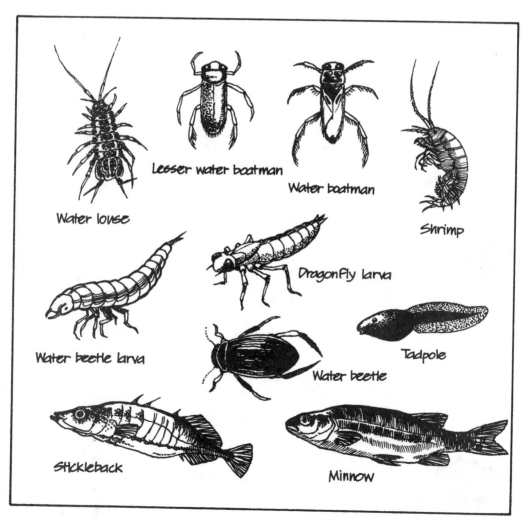

Water louse

Lesser water boatman

Water boatman

Shrimp

Water beetle larva

Dragonfly larva

Water beetle

Tadpole

Stickleback

Minnow

Fishing a midge pupa

This artificial is meant to represent the pupae of chironomidae (midges) which hang in the surface film before their final metamorphosis into the adult midge (buzzer).

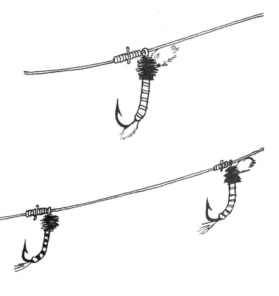

To ensure that the artificial hangs stationary in the surface film, the leader should be greased so that it floats. Mount two or three on the leader, each one stopped by a blood knot. Tie a sedge, well treated with floatant, on the point to act as an additional buoy.

Set-up for fishing pupae near the bottom.

Strike when the sedge disappears.

Midge pupae can also be fished in the traditional style, and retrieved very slowly.

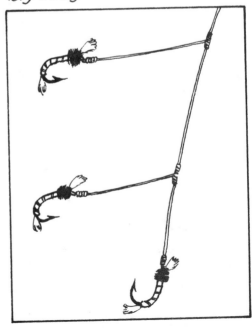

Fishing a sedge pupa

This pattern is a general representation of the many different sedge pupae found in most stillwaters. During the summer months, the natural swims to the surface, or to the shore, in order to undergo the final transformation and become an adult sedge fly.

The artificial can be fished at mid-water, or near the bottom with a sinking line ....

.... or just under the surface with a floating, sink-tip, or very slow-sinking line.

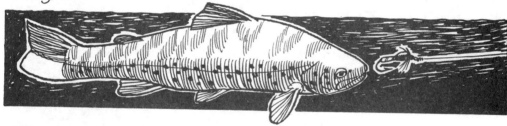

Retrieve the pupa at a medium pace, with long steady pulls, and a pause here and there.

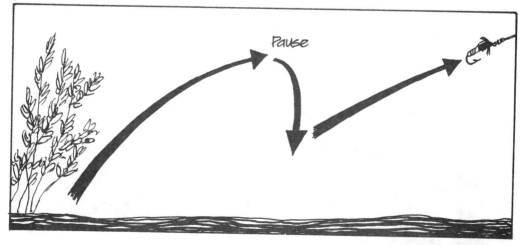

Pause

35

Fishing a damselfly nymph

During the early part of the season this pattern can be fished, very slowly, along the bottom. Shallower bays, where weed is prolific during the summer, are the most likely areas to attract the natural nymphs, as they feed largely on decaying vegetable matter.

During the warmer months the nymphs are far more active and wriggle to the surface, whereupon they proceed to swim towards the shore or surface weed in order to hatch into adult damselflies. To simulate this activity, fish the artificial just under the surface with a fairly fast retrieve, on a floating line.

Where there are rushes or reeds, it is often more productive to cast and retrieve along the shoreline.

Fishing a daddy-long-legs

The crane fly or 'daddy-long-legs' is a familiar sight at the water-side from June onwards. They are often blown onto the water surface where they struggle in their attempts to become air-borne once more. Such a large insect presents a good mouthful to the trout, which respond avidly.

Cast the artificial to an area where trout activity is obvious on the surface, (the fly will need to be well 'dunked' in floatant), then just wait for a fish to find it.

When a take does occur, resist the temptation to strike, as the trout will often try to drown the fly first, before taking it in its mouth.

Wait until the line starts to run out, then lift the rod high to set the hook.

Drag a 'daddy-long-legs' through a heavy ripple, or waves, and the trout will often respond with a very positive take.

Fishing a corixa

This pattern imitates the lesser water-boatman which spends most of its life near the bed of the lake, but has to rise to the surface in order to replenish its air supply.

Two patterns have developed to represent this little bug. The leaded version, which can be fished via a floating or a sinking line close to the bottom...

... and the buoyant (plastazote) version, which has to be fished with a sinking line.

Cast the buoyant corixa and allow the line to sink—the corixa will float on or near the surface.

When the line is retrieved, the corixa will dive towards the bottom, imitating, in a very life-like manner, the action of a water-boatman as it swims back to base.

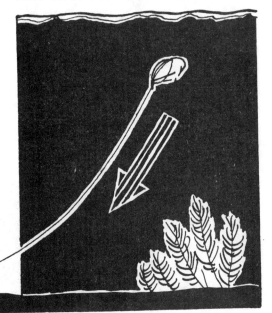

Fishing a leaded shrimp

This pattern represents the fresh-water shrimp, Gammarus; a resident of well-oxygenated water. They thrive in watercress, suggesting therefore that lakes fed by streams containing this plant would be ideal places to use this very effective little pattern.

The combination of lead wire and the shape of the body results in the artificial adopting an inverted attitude, which simulates the natural in a very life-like manner.

A leaded shrimp is ideally suited for margin fishing in clear-water lakes. Let the shrimp sink to the bottom where trout are patrolling.

When a trout approaches, inch the shrimp off the bottom in short jerks.

River and stream fishing

Trout can be found in most rivers and streams where the water is clean. The trout of the fast rocky streams of the higher ground are usually small in comparison to the fish of the lowland rivers. Because of the turbulent nature of the rocky stream, wet fly fishing is the method most widely employed. On the lowland river, where the flow is more sedate, the dry fly is favoured.

Moorland stream

Lowland stream

River and stream fishing

There is no need for a heavy line when fishing a stream. No's. 4,5 or 6 will be ideal. A light coloured line will show up far better in the shadows of overhanging foliage.

Other items needed will include; waders, strong tackle bag with a wide shoulder strap, collapsible landing net, priest, fly floatant, leader sink (if nymph fishing), scissors, spare leaders and a selection of flies.

River and stream fishing

The successful river fly-fisherman is the one who moves with stealth, and remains outside the trout's field of vision.

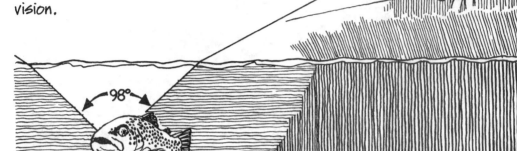

It is obvious from the above diagram that the only blind spot is directly to the rear of the trout. Whenever possible, approach the fish from that direction; especially when fishing in a confined area such as is commonly encountered on small overgrown streams.

In very clear water, a trout lying near the river bed will have a larger field of vision than a trout lying near the surface.

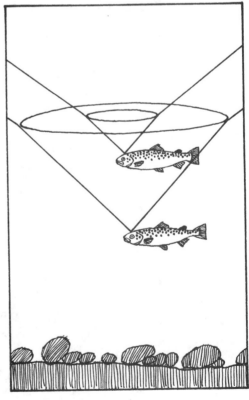

Drab clothing merges with the background, and aids concealment, even when the angler is in the trout's field of vision.

Olive-green, waxed cotton jackets, or army surplus combat jackets are ideal.

It is often necessary to wade, even on small streams. Again, olive-green is the best colour to choose for waders, and they should not have studs. A better grip may be provided by studs on some surfaces, but they produce such a clatter on stones and pebbles that the trout can detect the vibration yards away.

Waders with cleated rubber soles are best for stalking trout.

Concealment

The ideal position to be in, when wading a pool, is tucked away under the bank. For safety's sake, always tread very carefully; even small streams contain deep and sudden drop-offs into nasty holes. There is nothing as effective as a wader full of water for dampening the spirits.

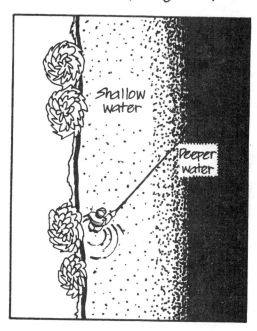

Shallow water

Deeper water

FIRM SILT OR SAND — The ideal material for wading on; muffles sound very efficiently.

ROCK — Cleated soles are silent on this, but it can be slippery.

PEBBLES — The worst base for stalking on. It is very noisy and sends shock waves right through a pool.

Fly presentation

When fishing in the confines of an overgrown stream the overhead cast is seldom practical. Instead, use the side cast.

The principal and timing of the side cast are the same as those of the overhead cast.

Pause

Work the line on an imaginary plane between overhanging foliage and the water surface.

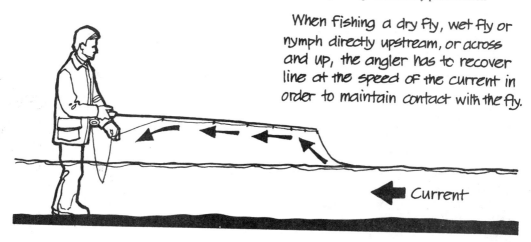

When fishing a dry fly, wet fly or nymph directly upstream, or across and up, the angler has to recover line at the speed of the current in order to maintain contact with the fly.

Current

When fishing from the bank on a small stream, with a short line on the water, the same effect can be achieved by moving the rod.

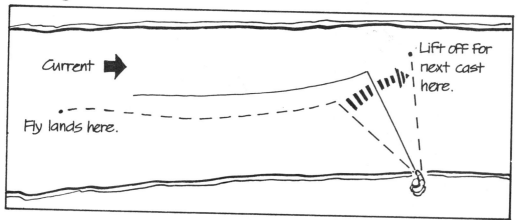

Current

Fly lands here.

Lift off for next cast here.

Presentation of a floating fly directly downstream.

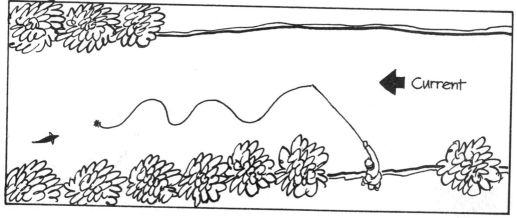

Current

Trout in a river always lie with their heads facing upstream, so it therefore makes sense to approach them from the rear, gradually working your way upstream.

A correctly-presented fly should alight, gently, just ahead of the rising trout. If the fly lands too far ahead of the trout, the line may fall into the trout's field of vision.

Dry fly presentation

When you have to fish across the stream to the trout, you should have no problem as long as the flow is even from bank to bank.

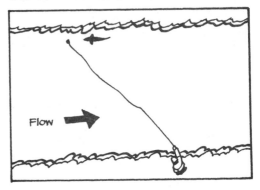

Unfortunately, conditions do not always present a perfect situation.

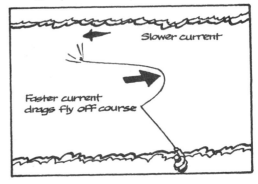

The remedy for this is to create some slack line.

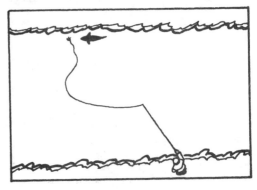

Dry fly presentation

When two or more trout are rising in close proximity to one another, care must be taken to select the fish in the correct order, to avoid scaring the other fish.

There are occasions when rises are few and far between, but this does not mean efforts with the dry fly will prove fruitless. Cover every likely-looking spot with a cast or two, and be prepared for a take just as if you had cast to a rising fish. Here are some places worth trying.

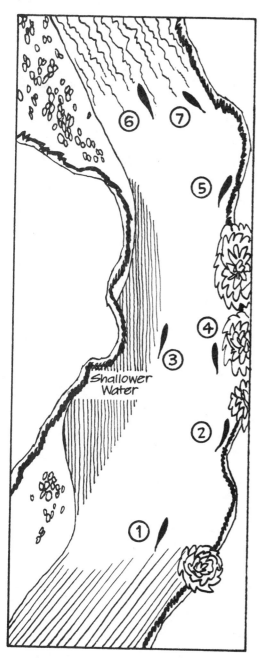

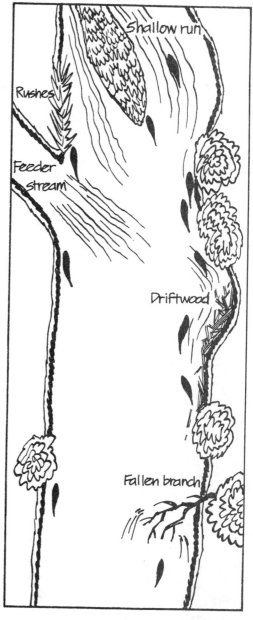

Upstream wet fly

Smaller, fast-flowing, overgrown streams are ideally suited to the upstream wet fly method.

Trout lies in a small rocky river

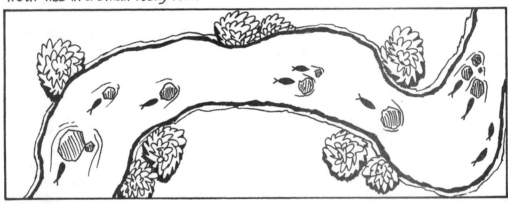

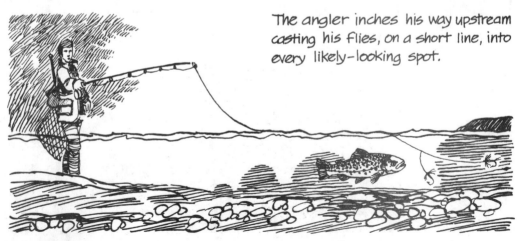

The angler inches his way upstream casting his flies, on a short line, into every likely-looking spot.

The downstream method

This method is practised with a team of, usually, three flies, similar to that used in the traditional loch method, but using smaller patterns. It is best employed on the larger, swiftly-flowing rocky rivers.

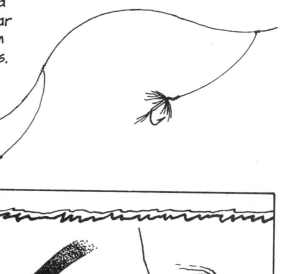

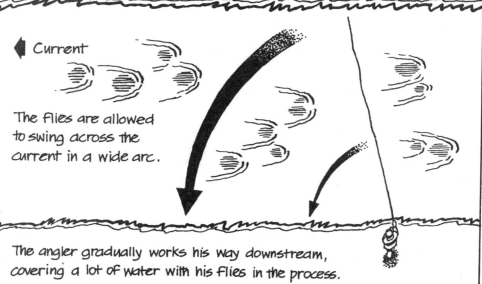

Current

The flies are allowed to swing across the current in a wide arc.

The angler gradually works his way downstream, covering a lot of water with his flies in the process.

Pay special attention to the quieter water on the downstream side of large stones.

Presenting a nymph in running water

The more sedate flow of the low-land river is ideally suited to fishing a nymph. Nymph fishing comes into its own when the trout are not feeding on the imago, but are intercepting the nymph as it swims to the surface or is being carried along in the flow of the current. If trout are 'bulging' just beneath the surface, or are showing their tails, then this is the time to tie on a nymph.

The artificial nymph is fished singly and cast upstream; in fact, the whole procedure is like dry fly fishing, except that here the nymph is meant to sink as soon as it hits the water. In nymph fishing, the avoidance of drag is not important. Nymphs are free-swimming and the trout take them as they swim in all directions.

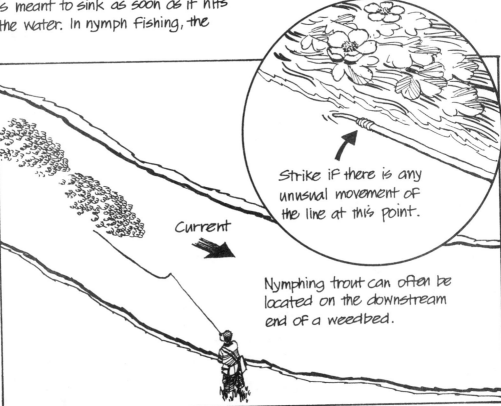

Current

Strike if there is any unusual movement of the line at this point.

Nymphing trout can often be located on the downstream end of a weedbed.

Small stream dapping

On many small streams bank-side foliage is so dense as to make orthodox fly presentation impossible. However, the angler who uses a little initiative and stealth, can extract trout that would make the locals gasp with astonishment.

The angler should walk slowly and quietly along the bank, or sit in a position which affords a reasonable view of the water. Eventually a trout will show itself by rising.

The angler should then take up a position directly over the fish. Concealment and stealth are now even more important. The rod is poked through the foliage and the fly lowered until it touches the surface of the water. Some movement can be imparted to the fly by jiggling the rod-tip.

When the trout takes the fly, the rod-tip should be lowered before lifting into the fish.

A long-handled net is almost always necessary to extract trout from these confined places.

Ideal patterns for stream dapping.

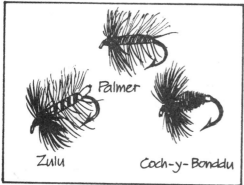

Palmer

Zulu

Coch-y-Bonddu

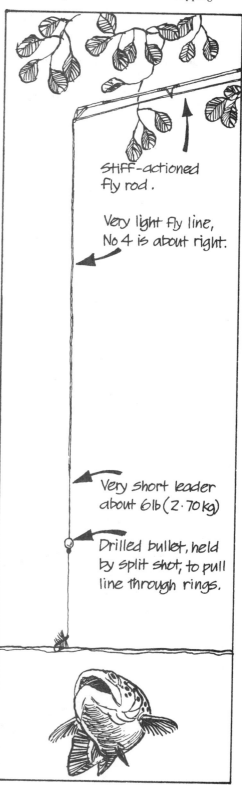

Stiff-actioned fly rod.

Very light fly line, No 4 is about right.

Very short leader about 6lb (2.70 kg)

Drilled bullet, held by split shot, to pull line through rings.

Hooking

A trout taking a wet fly fished downstream in fast water will often hook itself. The angler feels the tug and the fish is on.

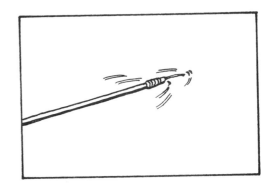

The take of a trout that has just accepted an upstream wet fly or a nymph is far more subtle. The best way to detect these invisible takes is to watch the point where the line joins the leader. When a take occurs the line will stop, or be drawn upstream. Then is the time to tighten on the fish.

A small trout snatching at a dry fly in a fast stream needs to be struck very quickly, by flicking back the wrist.

Larger trout in slower, quieter water should be allowed to turn well down with the fly; in fact, it is often advisable to wait until the line starts to move forward. This is particularly important on the majority of still-waters.

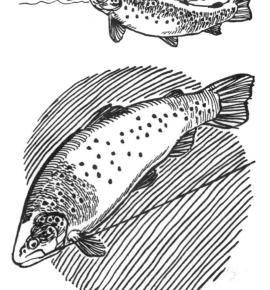

Playing and landing on rivers

Once the hook is set, the rod-tip should be held well up. A small trout dashing around a pool in a moorland stream should prove no problem; the elasticity of the rod-tip will absorb its activity until it is ready for the net. Larger trout, however, will have to be given some line, but with a steady strain applied.

Some anglers play a trout from the reel, while others prefer to control the fish via the line.

The rod-tip should be held well up.

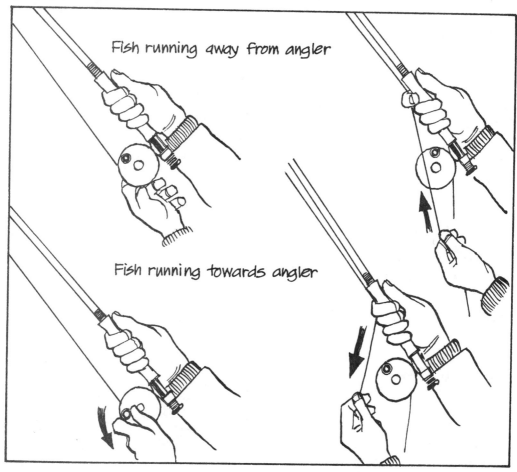

Fish running away from angler

Fish running towards angler

A fish heading for snags can be turned by applying side strain.

Never attempt to net a trout before it has tired sufficiently to be controlled under the rod-tip. Adopt as low a profile as possible and avoid all unnecessary movement. Draw the fish over the stationary net. Never jab at the fish in an attempt to scoop it out.

For heavy trout, lift the net from the water using the following procedure.

Etiquette

When fishing on the bank of a lake, always position yourself at a respectable distance from the next occupied bank space.

When approaching an angler who is in the process of casting, give him a wide berth, or wait until he has completed the cast before you pass him by.

When boat fishing keep well away from other boats.

If another angler is fishing your favourite pool on the river, wait until he moves on, or walk a good distance either up or down stream before you commence fishing.

Introduction to Stillwater Trout Fishing

Stillwater trout fishing can, by and large, be divided into two types. First, there is the abundance of naturally occurring lakes and lochs containing natural brown trout, of which the Irish and Scottish lochs are the most famous and highly regarded. Second, there are the reservoirs and purpose-made fisheries. These rely on the artificial stocking of rainbows, to keep up the quantity of trout necessary to attract the modern angler who, in return for his or her money, expects at least a sporting chance of catching a decent fish.

The fisheries stocked with rainbow trout have come a long way since Blagdon became the first reservoir in the UK to be stocked with rainbows back in 1904. No better choice of reservoir could have been made and it soon became evident that not only did the newcomers flourish but they also co-habited harmoniously with the native brown trout. From that date onwards, the foundations were laid for the stillwater trout fishing that we cherish and enjoy today.

Tony Whieldon illustrates all the basic knowledge needed by the angler taking up fishing for trout with the fly, whatever type of stillwater he or she is fishing on. However, as any experienced angler will tell you, there is no substitute for actually getting out on the water to fish and to observe other anglers.

Some will be the clever ones, others will have that natural knack to be at one with nature; then there are those who think they are clever. Finally, there is the majority: anglers who use their commonsense and work hard to improve their fishing skills, loving every minute of it, and revelling in every day that they guess right or recognize some small point that has escaped the attention of other anglers.

It would be easy for me to describe at length the traditional joys of presenting a diminutive dry fly and that heart-pounding moment as a trout sips the delicate concoction of fur and feather, which has been so lovingly tied during those dark winter evenings when the wind and rain lashed against the window-panes. It is right that this aspect of fly fishing should be mentioned because no one can truly be called a fly fisherman or woman unless they have tied at least some of their own flies.

Perhaps this is where stillwater trout fishing begins to demand special skills because, although the traditional dry and wet fly skills of the river fisherman overlap and transfer easily to stillwater angling, the stillwater trout angler has evolved fly patterns and skills peculiar to stillwaters, and in particular to the rainbow trout.

A number of these flies and methods do not sit at all easily with the traditional flyfishing purist! Nevertheless, like it or not, they are now part and parcel of today's flyfishing scene. Some of these flies are more akin to spinning lures than flies, and the heavy rods and lines necessary to cast them would not be out of place in pursuit of fish many times the weight of the average stillwater trout. However, that said, there is now a perceptible and welcome trend back towards the lighter rod and line weight.

Author Tony Whieldon is an angler who by far prefers the joy of deceiving a trout with the cunning of expert fly-tying and delicacy of presentation, rather than the repetitive long casting and fast retrieve of the habitual lure fisherman.

Tony has succeeded in capturing, within these pages, a distillation of the fishing skills that are needed for the different types of stillwaters, and which so many of us work so hard to acquire. His finely tuned sense of observation, which in no small way contributes to his talent as an artist, also makes him a joy to fish with. His understanding of flyfishing techniques and his ability to draw them in a clear and sympathetic way combine to make a text which is clear and yet comprehensible. This section points the way for those that want to learn the essential stillwater skills, as I have learned by fishing with him.

Russell Symons,
Plymouth, Devon.

Lake fishing

Protective clothing is of vital importance to the angler who fishes the exposed banks of large stillwater fisheries.

A waxed proofed cotton jacket complete with hood and storm collar will keep the elements at bay. Thigh waders will keep the legs warm and dry. Make sure that the jacket hangs well down over the top of the waders.

The tackle bag should be large and roomy to accommodate, apart from spare reels etc., the large fly box which is necessary to hold the comprehensive selection of flies and lures that is required for lake fishing.

Lake fishing

The expanse of an unfamiliar lake may pose a problem to a visiting angler, but if he applies his knowledge and experience of other lakes to this one, he will soon locate fish. For every lake, whether it is man-made or natural, has features in common with other lakes, as well as its own personal characteristics. Here are some places well worth attention.

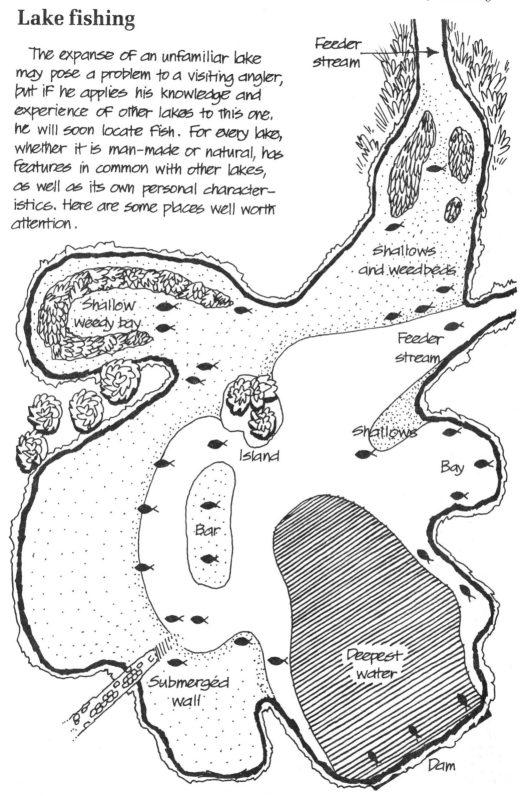

Feeder stream

shallows and weedbeds

Shallow weedy bay

Feeder stream

Shallows

Island

Bay

Bar

Submerged wall

Deepest water

Dam

Stillwaters

WILD MOORLAND LAKES

RESERVOIRS

SMALL MAN-MADE FISHERIES

Weather – the effects of wind

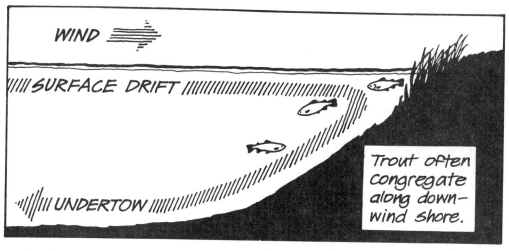

Using the wind

The wind can often be of assistance in the location of fish. Warm
winds from the south, and south-
west are best, both for fish and
fishermen.

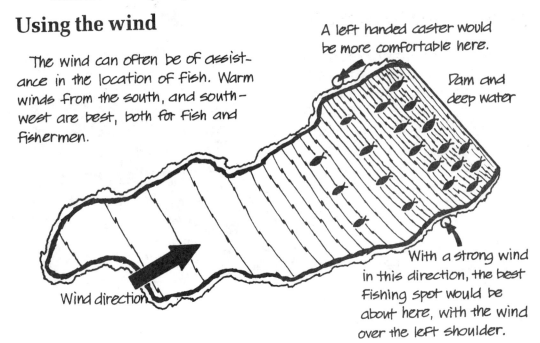

A left handed caster would
be more comfortable here.

Dam and
deep water

With a strong wind
in this direction, the best
fishing spot would be
about here, with the wind
over the left shoulder.

Wind direction

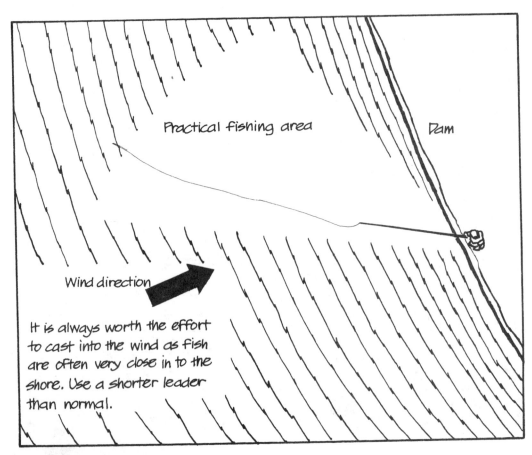

Practical fishing area

Dam

Wind direction

It is always worth the effort
to cast into the wind as fish
are often very close in to the
shore. Use a shorter leader
than normal.

Lake fishing from the bank

When fish are showing on the surface, they are usually feeding on
insects which have been blown on to
the water surface from the shore,
or on nymphs or pupae hanging in
the surface film.

If there are a number of fish
rising fairly close together, cast
among them and work the fly back
slowly in very short jerks.

Method of retrieving a small fly or
or nymph with a floating line.

63

Fishing a lure from the bank

Hungry, early-season trout will grab almost any lure that is cast into a lake. Some lakes at this time of year tend to carry a certain amount of colour, which demands the use of a high-visibility lure, such as a Jack Frost, Appetizer, Ace of Spades or Dog Nobbler.

As the season advances, however, the food supply is more abundant, and the trout become more selective. Nymphs and flies are then the main items of food, but where fish fry exist these are also taken, and it is possible to imitate them with a lure. The shallows of many lakes support a healthy population of sticklebacks, minnows and other small fry on which the trout feed.

High visibility lures

Jack Frost Appetizer

Ace of Spades Missionary

Fry imitators

Polystickle

Church Fry

Jersey Herd

Sinfoil's Fry

Where fry activity is seen, cast a fry lure along the shore-line.

Fishing a lure from the bank

The Dog Nobbler is rather unusual inasmuch as it carries a whole split-shot as part of its dressing. It certainly does not represent anything in particular, but when drawn through the water it has a very stimulating action.

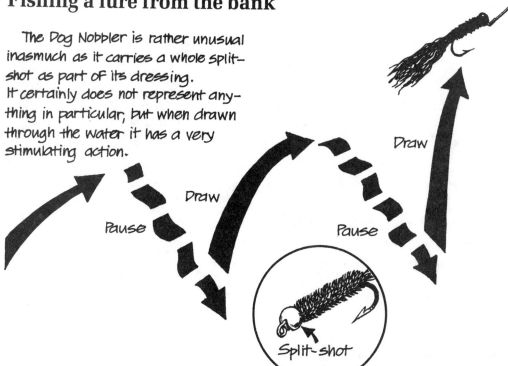

Draw

Pause

Draw

Pause

Draw

Split-shot

Another unique lure is the Muddler Minnow, which has the tendency to float, rather than sink like the Dog Nobbler. In medium-depth water it works better on a floating line; but in deep water, a slow-sinking line is more suitable if the fish are swimming deeper.

Lake fishing from a boat

The traditional loch style of fishing from a drifting boat is still very widely practised, and accounts for many good fish.

Bob Fly

Point fly

Middle dropper

The team of flies is cast ahead of the drifting boat on a fairly short line, and retrieved by lifting the rod.

A zulu is an ideal pattern to use as a bob fly, and if possible it should be made to dribble through the surface during the retrieve.

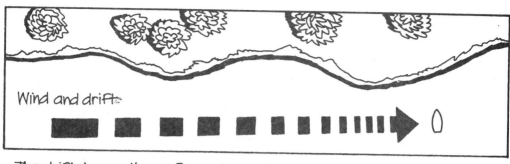

Wind and drift

The drift is usually performed along, and not too far out from, the shore-line. When the boat is drifting too quickly a drogue can be used to check its progress.

Drift →

Suggested patterns and positions

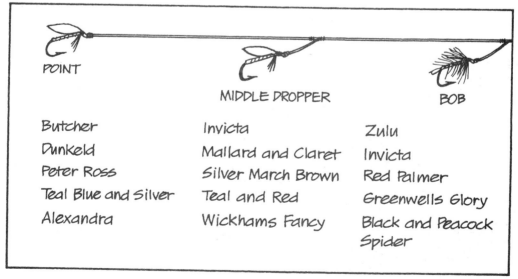

POINT	MIDDLE DROPPER	BOB
Butcher	Invicta	Zulu
Dunkeld	Mallard and Claret	Invicta
Peter Ross	Silver March Brown	Red Palmer
Teal Blue and Silver	Teal and Red	Greenwells Glory
Alexandra	Wickhams Fancy	Black and Peacock Spider

Lake fishing from a boat

Casting a dry fly to rising trout is a delightful form of boat-fishing.

This is particularly effective when flies, especially hawthorn flies and crane flies, are being blown on to the lake from the shore.

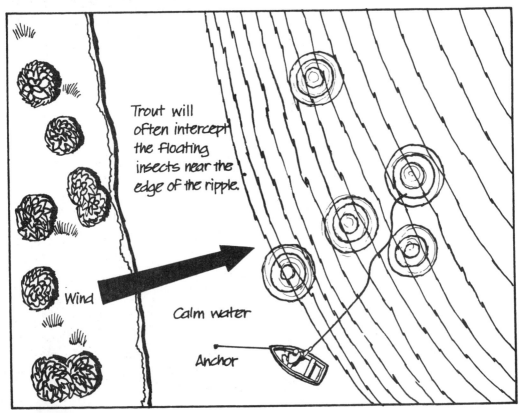

Trout will often intercept the floating insects near the edge of the ripple.

Wind

Calm water

Anchor

Dapping with a daddy-long-legs

Dapping with a natural daddy-long-legs has been a method of angling practised for many years, on some Irish and Scottish lochs.

Given the right conditions, this form of fishing can be applied to most stillwater fisheries. There is no need to use the natural insect either—an artificial 'daddy' works just as well.

The boat is allowed to drift before the wind, just as with the loch-style of wet fly fishing. The rod, however, needs to be as long as possible in order to present plenty of line to the wind.

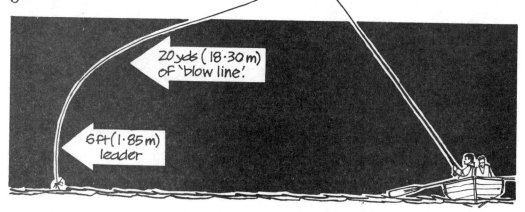

20 yds (18·30 m) of 'blow line'

6 ft (1·85 m) leader

Simply let the line blow out over the water, and attempt to keep the fly dancing in the waves.

With this method, an over-hasty strike will result in a missed fish. Wait until the trout has turned down with the fly in its mouth, then just tighten up.

Lure fishing from a boat is undoubtably a very productive form of trout fishing. A single lure can be fished just beneath the surface, at mid-water, or on the bottom.

Lure fishing from a boat

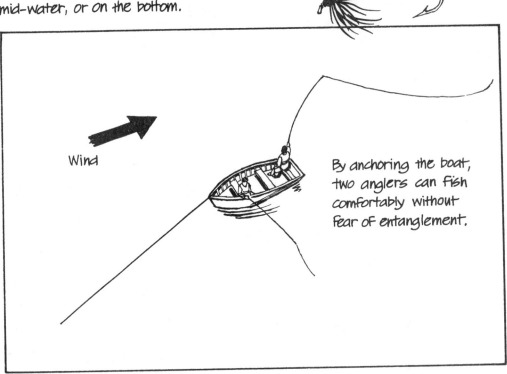

Wind

By anchoring the boat, two anglers can fish comfortably without fear of entanglement.

Expect a take at any time, even when the retrieve has almost finished. Some really vicious takes occur when the lure is close under the boat.

Trolling

This method involves trailing a lure about 30–40 yd (28–36 m) behind a rowing boat. A lead core line is used to keep the lure well down in the water. Lures used for this sort of fishing are usually of the tandem variety.

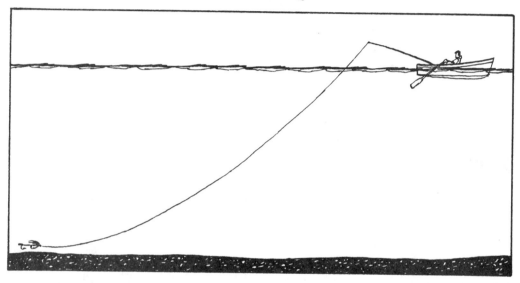

Trout caught with this method are generally larger than average.

Stillwater rods

RODS

(A) 9ft 6in (2·90m) carbon rod with a line rating of 7-9 for bank fishing and lure fishing from a boat.

(B) 11ft (3·35m) carbon rod with a line rating of 5-7 for loch-style fishing from a drifting boat.

(C) 7ft (2·15m) carbon rod with a line rating of 4-5 for floating line work from bank or boat.

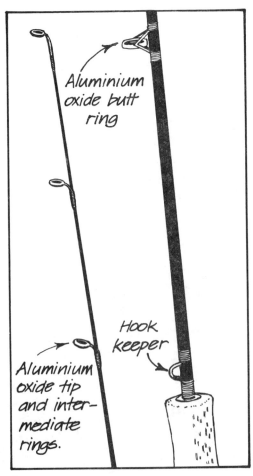

Aluminium oxide butt ring

Hook keeper

Aluminium oxide tip and intermediate rings.

Stillwater reels

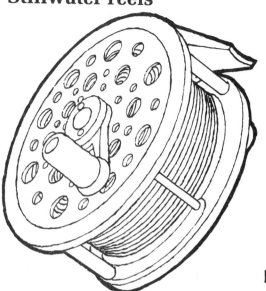

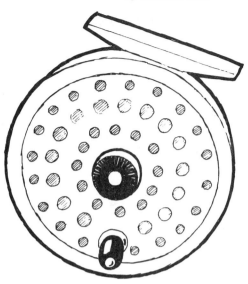

Wide drum multiplier reel with line and backing for use with the 9ft 6in(2·90m) rod.

Lightweight magnesium, single action reel holding a 4-5 line, for use with the 7ft(2·15m) carbon rod.

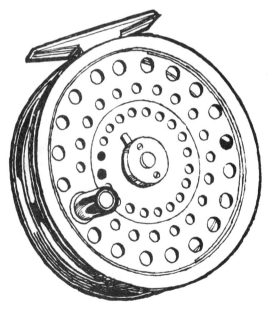

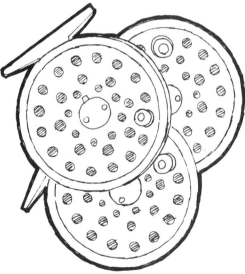

Standard drum, single action reel holding 5-7 double taper floating line for use with the 11ft (3·35m) loch-style rod.

A selection of lines loaded on to spare spools or reels will be needed for the 9ft6in (2·90m) rod. eg., WF Floater, WF Sinker, or Shooting Head Floater and Sinker and DT Floater.

The stillwater trout's diet

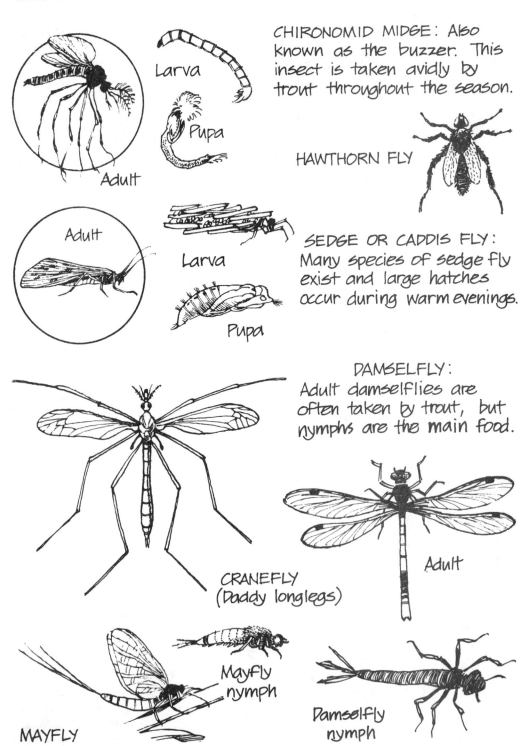

Larva

Pupa

Adult

CHIRONOMID MIDGE: Also known as the buzzer. This insect is taken avidly by trout throughout the season.

HAWTHORN FLY

Adult

Larva

Pupa

SEDGE OR CADDIS FLY: Many species of sedge fly exist and large hatches occur during warm evenings.

DAMSELFLY: Adult damselflies are often taken by trout, but nymphs are the main food.

Adult

CRANEFLY (Daddy longlegs)

Mayfly nymph

MAYFLY

Damselfly nymph

Changes through the year

Early season

As some small, stillwater fisheries remain open the whole year through (there is no close season for rainbow trout) the angler could well be casting his flies on New Year's Day; an early start indeed!

The best approach at this time of year is to fish the fly or flies in the deepest area of the lake, close to the bottom.

EARLY SEASON FLIES

VIVA

JACK FROST

MONTANA NYMPH

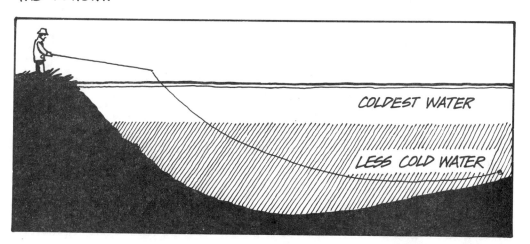

COLDEST WATER

LESS COLD WATER

SHELTERING FROM EARLY-SEASON COLD WINDS

Weed growth is minimal at this time of year and flies can be retrieved slowly, close to the lake bed.

However, a quick inspection of the hook is advisable after every cast as bits of detritus have a habit of becoming impaled on the point.

Although the tucked half-blood knot (a) is reliable, and widely used, it does allow the fly to hinge into a fixed position which could result in bad presentation. Alternatives are the turle knot (b) and the loop (c), both of which hold the fly rigid. Small wire clips (d) are available and ideal for larger imitations.

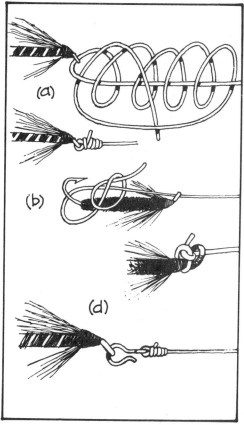

(a)

(b)

(d)

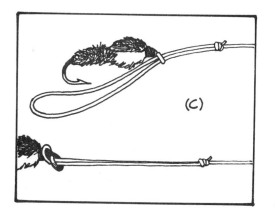

(c)

A pair of old leather gloves with the finger tips cut away provide protection for the hands during raw early-season conditions. A mere turn down of the wrist is all that is needed to keep the fly mobile.

Holding the rod tip at the correct level above the water surface will make visual take-detection easier.

Holding the rod at an angle to the line will lessen the risk of a snap-off if a trout makes a sudden hit-and-run attack.

12 in (30cm)

Warmer weather tactics

April and May (unless the winter has been extremely hard) will produce some tangible evidence that underwater life is astir after its winter dormancy. A floating line can now be used with confidence as trout will be more widespread.

Fishing with a floating line and a long leader, furnished with one, two or even three imitative patterns of under-water bug is usually referred to as nymph fishing, and is a very satisfying way of taking trout. However I feel that the angler should not develop a narrow-minded or puritanical attitude to this style, and should be prepared to use any concoction of fur and feather, within reason, and call it a nymph. After all, even the most delicate creations made at the fly-tying vice cannot compare with nature's ultra-fragile and translucent underwater creatures.

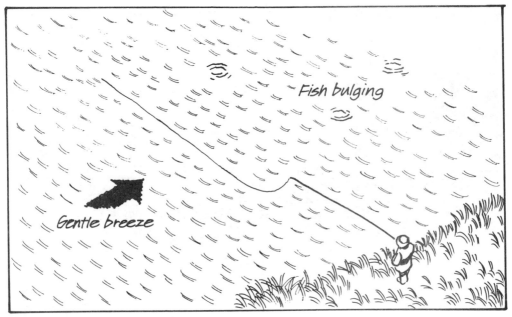

Fish bulging

Gentle breeze

IDEAL CONDITIONS FOR NYMPH FISHING

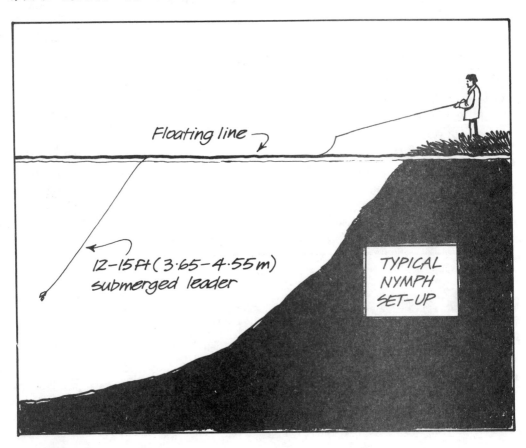

Floating line

12–15 ft (3·65–4·55 m) submerged leader

TYPICAL NYMPH SET-UP

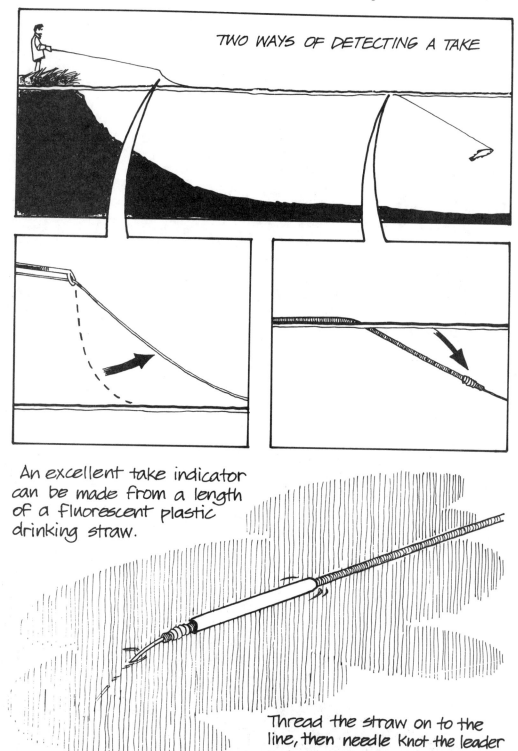

TWO WAYS OF DETECTING A TAKE

An excellent take indicator can be made from a length of a fluorescent plastic drinking straw.

Thread the straw on to the line, then needle knot the leader to hold the straw in place.

RETRIEVING A NYMPH

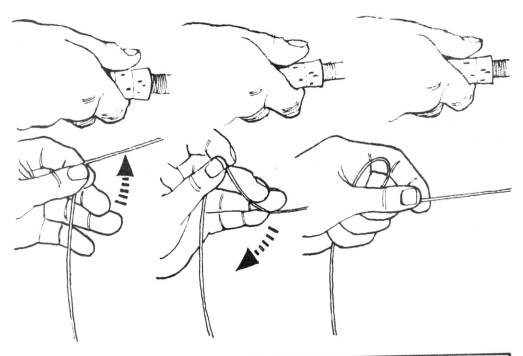

DRIFTING A NYMPH

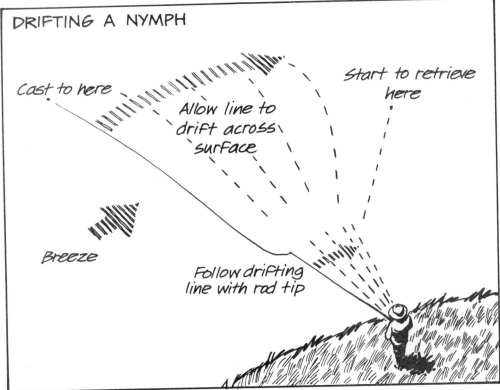

Cast to here

Allow line to drift across surface

Start to retrieve here

Breeze

Follow drifting line with rod tip

HOOK SIZES FOR DRIFTING A NYMPH

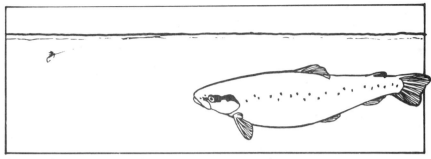

16-10

In or just beneath the surface film

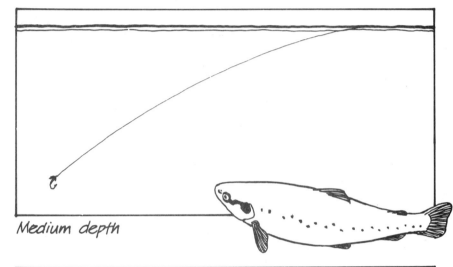

10-8

Medium depth

8-6
or smaller,
weighted
patterns

Deep

Retrieved or drifted nymphs
can also be very effective
using the dropper system.

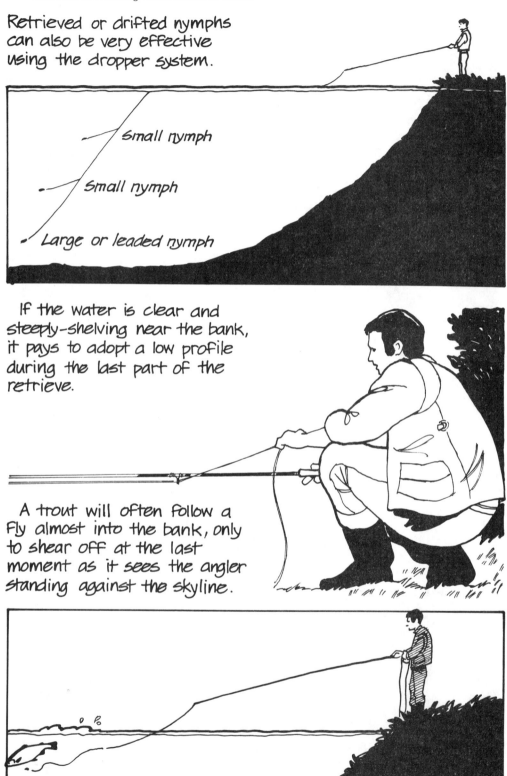

Small nymph

Small nymph

Large or leaded nymph

If the water is clear and
steeply-shelving near the bank,
it pays to adopt a low profile
during the last part of the
retrieve.

A trout will often follow a
fly almost into the bank, only
to shear off at the last
moment as it sees the angler
standing against the skyline.

Nymphs and pupae

Sedge Pupa

Midge Pupae

Damselfly Nymph

Amber Nymph

Montana Stone

Persuader

Iven's Nymph

Corixa

Mayfly Nymph

PVC Nymph

Cove's
Pheasant Tail

Damsel Wiggle Nymph

Leaded Shrimp

Pheasant Tail Nymph

Chompers

Collyer's Nymph

85

The magic of May

May produces the trout's first glut of food in the shape of the hawthorn fly (Bibio marci). This is a terrestrial insect, and at times the hatch is so prolific that dense clouds of the large black insect fill the air. Stocked fish which have been reared on a diet of high-protein pellets sample this feast, but it is the wild fish of the upland lakes and reservoirs that respond most avidly, packing on weight in a frenzy of feeding for a week or so until the hatch peters out. If the wind is favourable the hawthorns are blown on to the water and quickly devoured by the cruising trout.

Natural hawthorn fly and imitations

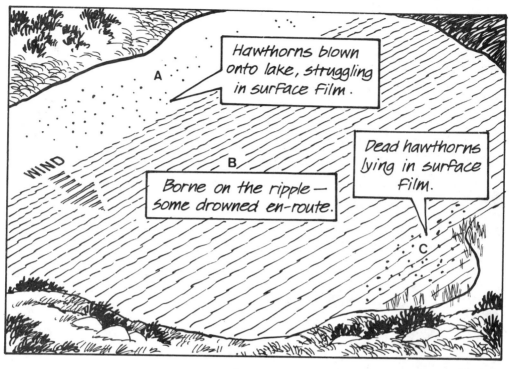

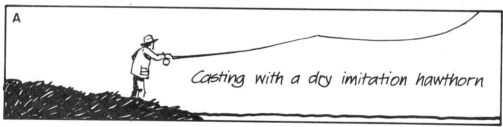

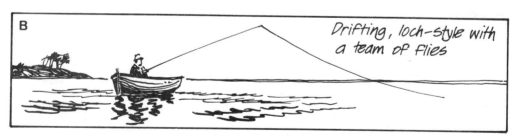

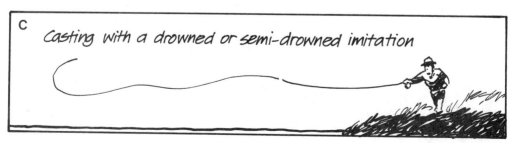

Back cast aimed high

Situation 'A' can present problems if the bank rises very steeply, so often the case on upland lakes. The best approach here is to use a long rod (the one recommended for loch-style boat fishing) and a double-taper 5-7 line. This outfit will reduce the number of hang-ups on gorse bushes, heather or bracken.

An alternative approach in this situation is to cast at an angle of about 45° to the shore. Trout will often be feeding fairly close in if the water is deep enough and many fish can be covered by working gradually along the bank.

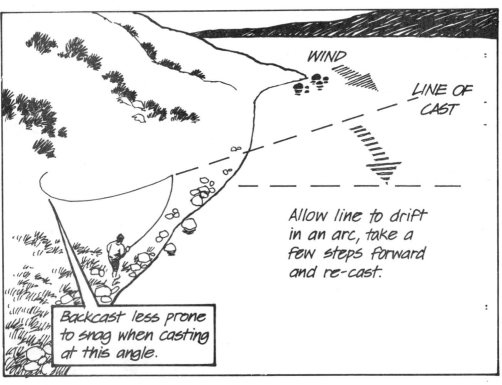

WIND

LINE OF CAST

Allow line to drift in an arc, take a few steps forward and re-cast.

Backcast less prone to snag when casting at this angle.

Dry flies

Black Gnat

Hawthorn

Hares Ear

Grey Duster

Knotted Midge

Alder

Coch-y-Bonddu

Baigent's Black

Walker's Sedge

G and H Sedge

Greenwell's Glory

Pheasant Tail

Daddy Longlegs

Coachman

Iron Blue Dun

Blue Upright

Dark Varient

Wickham's Fancy

Red Spinner

Silver Sedge

Loch-style

This popular, traditional method is performed by repeatedly casting a short line and a team of wet flies ahead of a drifting boat. May is an ideal month to start loch-style fishing, especially if the hawthorn fly is on the water.

① Using an 11ft (3·35 m) rod, cast a double-taper floating line, with a rating of 4–7, two rod lengths ahead of the boat.
② When the flies are in the water, lift the rod through an arc from A to B, thus imparting a smooth, continual retrieve to the flies. Keeping in touch with the flies by pulling line with the free hand may also be necessary.
③ Flick the line back and repeat the process.

POSITION AT POINT B

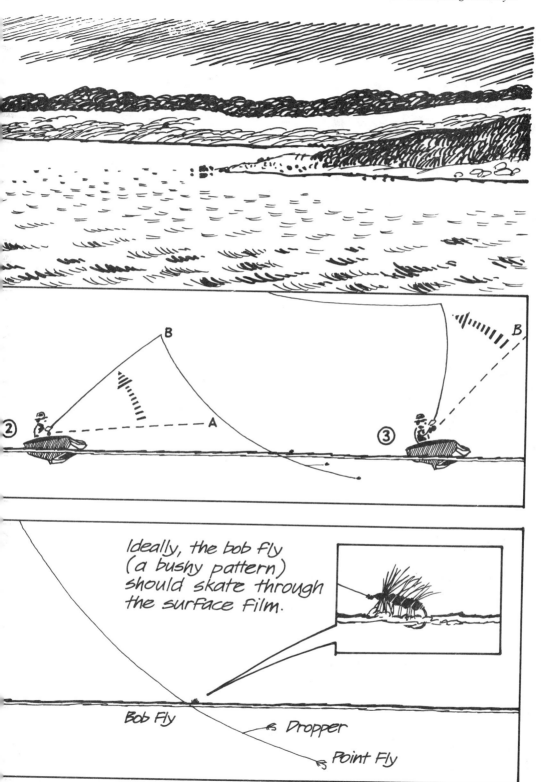

Ideally, the bob fly
(a bushy pattern)
should skate through
the surface film.

Bob Fly

Dropper

Point Fly

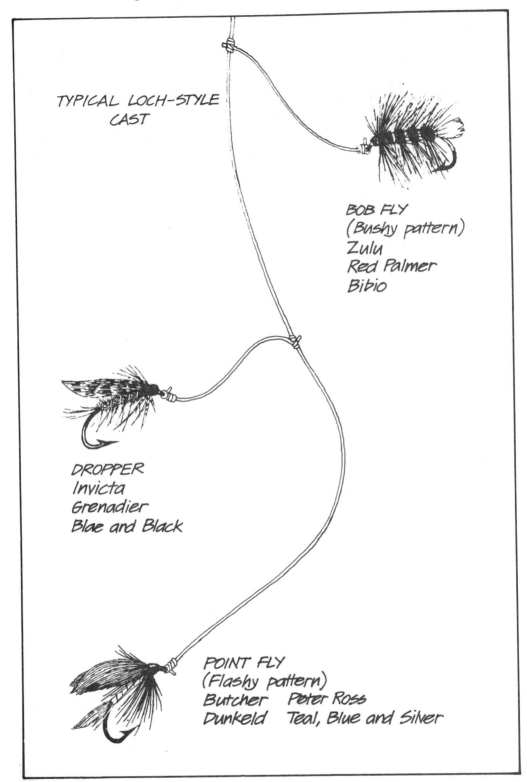

TYPICAL LOCH-STYLE
CAST

BOB FLY
(Bushy pattern)
Zulu
Red Palmer
Bibio

DROPPER
Invicta
Grenadier
Blae and Black

POINT FLY
(Flashy pattern)
Butcher   Peter Ross
Dunkeld   Teal, Blue and Silver

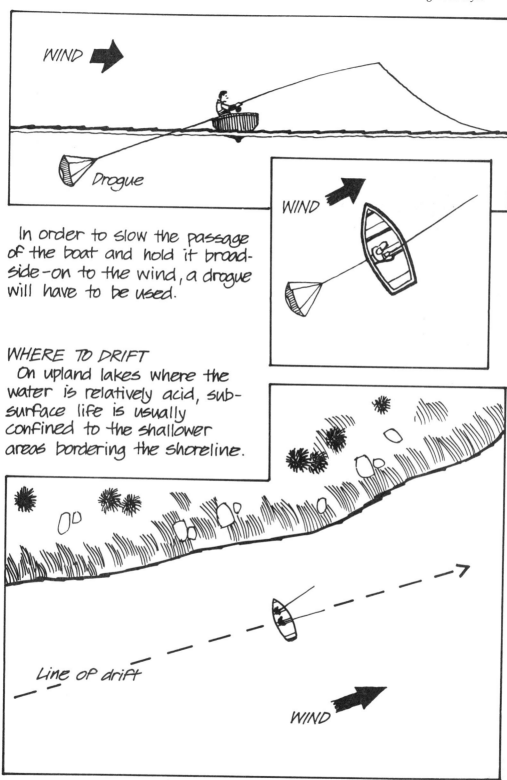

In order to slow the passage of the boat and hold it broadside-on to the wind, a drogue will have to be used.

WHERE TO DRIFT

On upland lakes where the water is relatively acid, subsurface life is usually confined to the shallower areas bordering the shoreline.

TYPICAL UPLAND LAKE

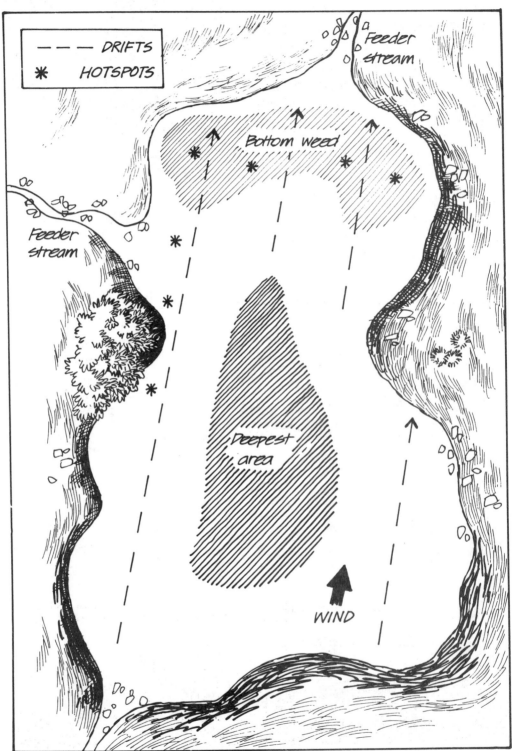

Lowland lakes with water having a more alkaline content will provide a larger choice of drifts as well as producing larger trout. However, the anomaly does present itself in some highland lochs, where the trout can average 2lb(0·90kg).

CHOICE OF LINE WEIGHT

With a gentle breeze, just enough to keep the boat moving, a No. 4 will provide perfect control.

Stronger blows will require heavier line such as No. 7.

WIND

DRIFT

The wind may not always be favourable for a natural drift, but with the aid of an experienced companion the boat can be held, by sculling the oars, so that it drifts parallel to the shoreline.

When a fish has been hooked, bring it around to the wind—ward side of the boat as soon as possible, where it can be played out and netted without the risk of the boat running over it.

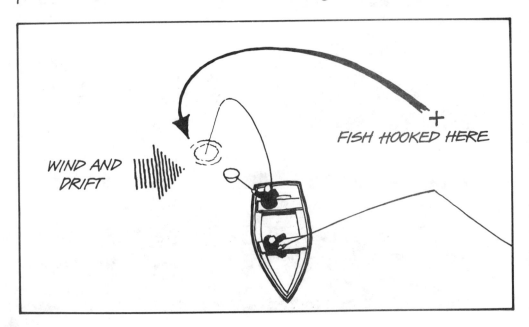

WIND AND DRIFT

FISH HOOKED HERE

Traditional wet flies

Butcher

Dunkeld

Black Zulu

Black and Peacock

Peter Ross

Invicta

Mallard and Claret

Grenadier

Silver March Brown

Black Spider

Teal and Red

Wickham's Fancy

Blae and Black

Teal and Green

Teal Blue and Silver

Alexandra

Coachman

Red Palmer

Parson Hughes

Black Pennell

97

Other boat fishing techniques

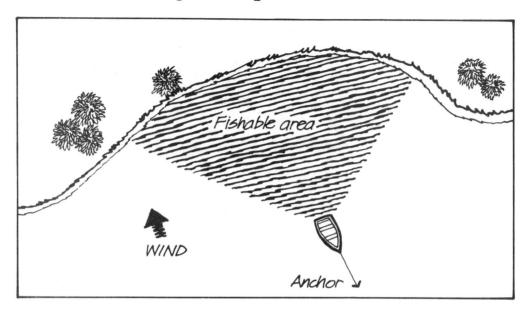

Small bays into which the wind is blowing are usually good fish-holding areas, especially if the lake bed supports any form of weed growth.

The loch-style outfit can be used here, although longer casts will be required. The flies should be retrieved nymph-style.

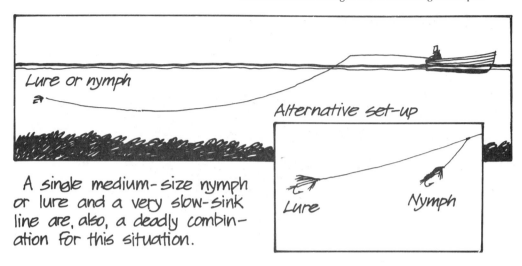

Lure or nymph

Alternative set-up

Lure   Nymph

A single medium-size nymph or lure and a very slow-sink line are, also, a deadly combination for this situation.

Lure fishing from a drifting boat

Although the traditional loch-style is the best method for catching fish which are near the surface, it is the deeply-presented lure that will score when trout are feeding closer to the lake bed.

PROCEDURE FOR FISHING A LURE FROM A DRIFTING BOAT

The boat is allowed to drift, with the aid of a rudder, bow first, downwind.

Each angler then casts, with a sinking line, at right angles to the boat.

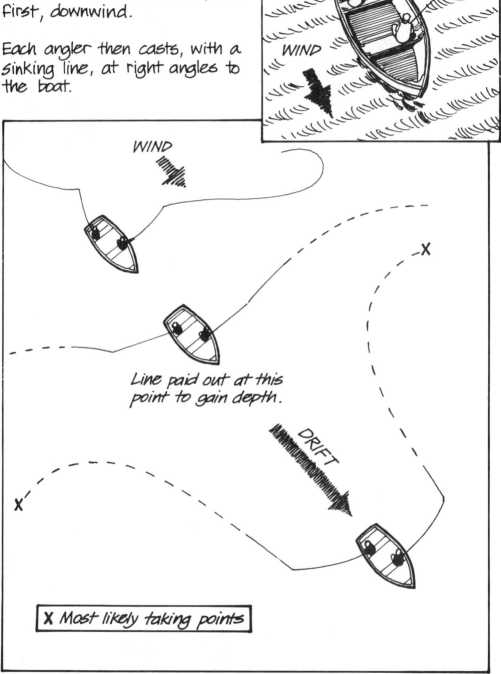

WIND

WIND

Line paid out at this point to gain depth.

DRIFT

X

X

X Most likely taking points

June, July and August

Early mornings, and evenings, provide the cream of the sport at this time of year, although excellent fishing can be had throughout the day if the sky is overcast.

Hatches of midge will be prolific, therefore it is logical to set up a rod in conjunction with a floating line and fish with an imitative pattern near the surface.

During periods of very hot, sunny weather it is wise to set up a standby rod which is equipped with a sinking line. This outfit can then be used if the fish retire to deeper water during the middle of the day.

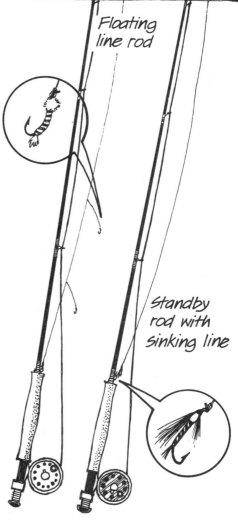

Floating line rod

Standby rod with sinking line

(A) On large reservoirs where the lake bed slopes gradually over large areas of shallows, long casts will be needed to cover midge-feeding trout. A floating weight-forward or shooting head line and a 9ft 6in (2.90m) carbon rod will be required here.

(B) Where trout are feeding closer to the shore the use of a double-taper line will be possible, allowing the angler to present the flies in a delicate manner.

(C) In certain situations, usually on small fisheries, trout will be feeding on midge pupae very close to the bank. A 7ft (2.15m) carbon rod and 4-5 double-taper line is the perfect combination for this exciting form of fishing.

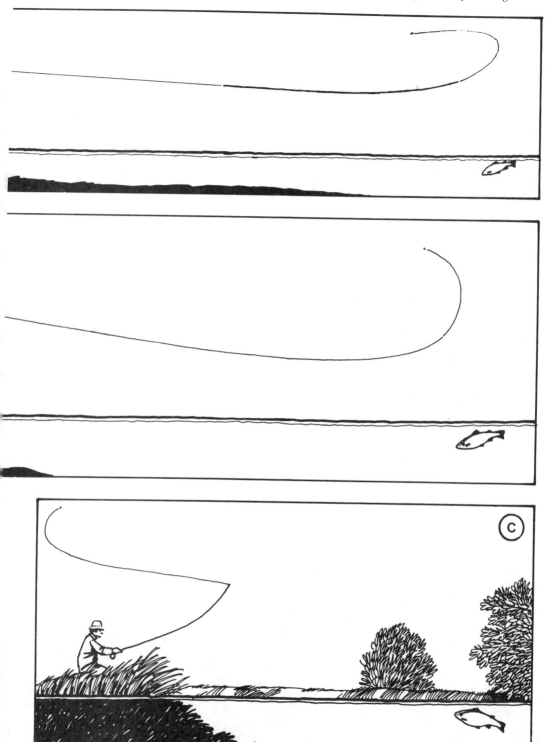

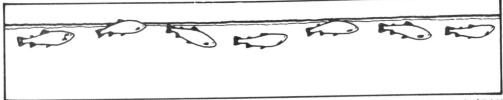

TYPICAL SWIMMING PATTERN OF A TROUT FEEDING ON MIDGE PUPAE

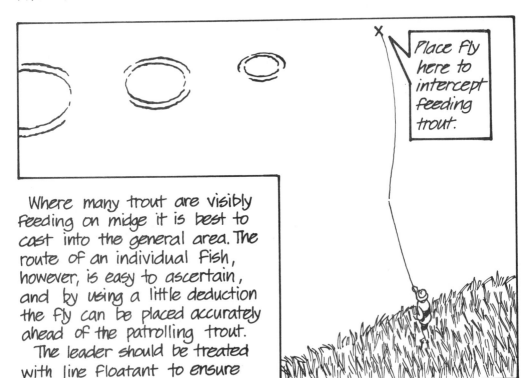

Place fly here to intercept feeding trout.

Where many trout are visibly feeding on midge it is best to cast into the general area. The route of an individual fish, however, is easy to ascertain, and by using a little deduction the fly can be placed accurately ahead of the patrolling trout.

The leader should be treated with line floatant to ensure that the artificial is presented where the trout expect to find it—

—in, or just under the surface film.

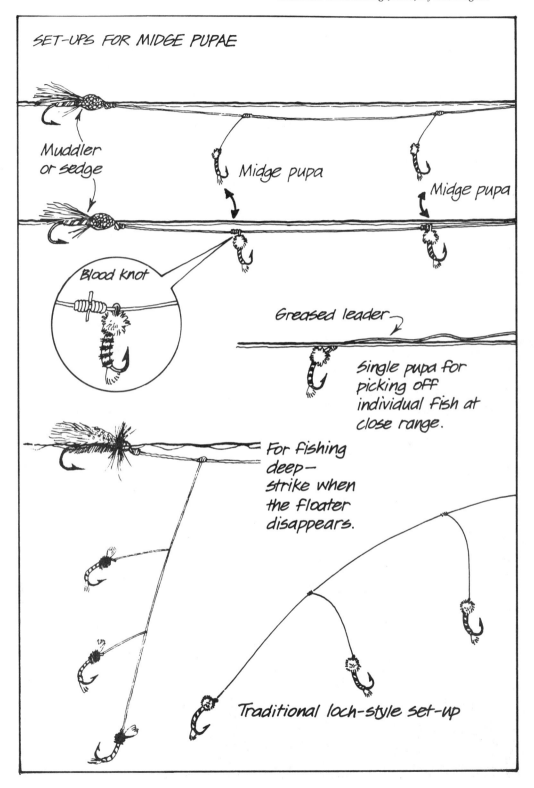

SET-UPS FOR MIDGE PUPAE

Muddler or sedge

Midge pupa

Midge pupa

Blood knot

Greased leader

Single pupa for picking off individual fish at close range.

For fishing deep— strike when the floater disappears.

Traditional loch-style set-up

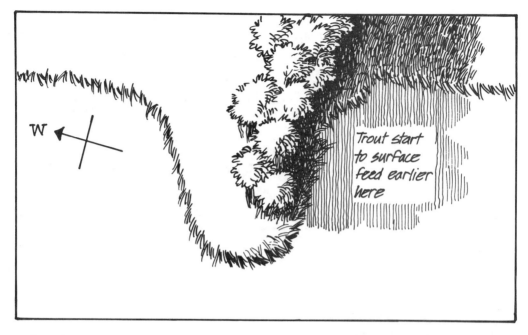

Trout start
to surface
feed earlier
here

W

Bright, calm sunny days during June, July and August do not provide ideal conditions for surface fishing. On such days, fishing deeply with a nymph or lure will be the only resort. However, midge and other insects continue to hatch, covering the surface with pupa, emerging adult insects and dead and dying terrestrial gnats and beetles.

Trout surface-feeding usually starts with the setting of the sun, but in areas of shadow on the east side of trees, it may start an hour earlier. Situations like this often provide the opportunity to indulge in some really close-in fishing with a light rod and line.

Bright, sunny days with a gentle, warm south-west or west wind provide a larder of insects in the surface film at the downwind end of a lake.

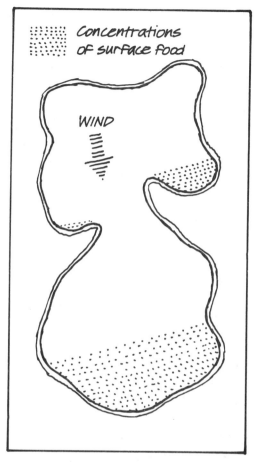

Concentrations of surface food

WIND

With the setting of the sun and the dying of the wind, trout will start to show in this area and will be easy to see against the backdrop of the sun's afterglow. A long rod and light line are the best combination for this situation, as it will often be an advantage, in the fading light, to lift the line off the water and cast quickly to a particular trout with the minimum of false casting.

There will be times when evening-rising trout seem to ignore tiny offerings such as artificial midge pupae. This can be extremely frustrating. However, it is probably due to the fact that the trout do not see the artificial. A lure such as a Sweeny Todd or a Viva, fished with a floating line and retrieved just beneath the surface, usually has the desired effect.

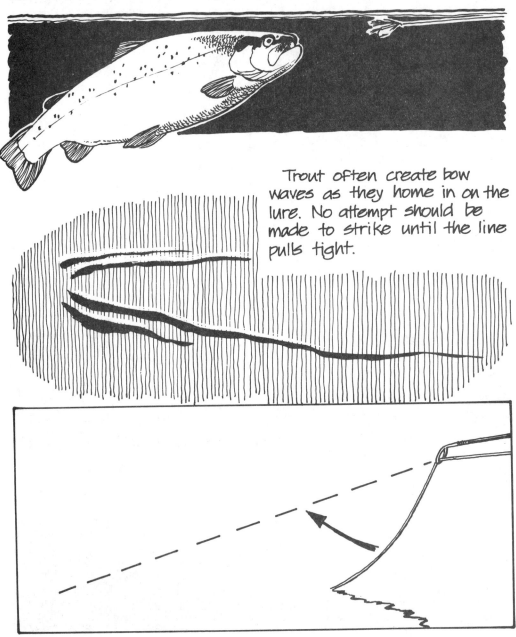

Trout often create bow waves as they home in on the lure. No attempt should be made to strike until the line pulls tight.

Warm summer evenings also provide the opportunity to fish a floating sedge imitation.

Sedge patterns can be fished static or drawn along the surface to assimilate the scuttling action of the natural insect.

Yet another effective fly to employ at dusk, or even after dark, if fishing is permitted, is a large white imitation ghost-swift moth.

G and H Sedge

Walker's Sedge

SUITABLE ARTIFICIAL SEDGES

Fishing a sedge pupa

This pattern is a general representation of the many different sedge pupae found in most stillwaters. During the summer months, the natural swims to the surface, or to the shore, in order to undergo the final transformation and become an adult sedge fly.

The artificial can be fished at midwater, or near the bottom with a sinking line . . . .

. . . . or just under the surface with a floating, sink-tip, or very slow-sinking line.

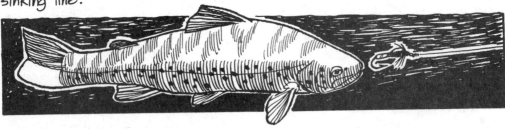

Retrieve the pupa at a medium pace, with long steady pulls, and a pause here and there.

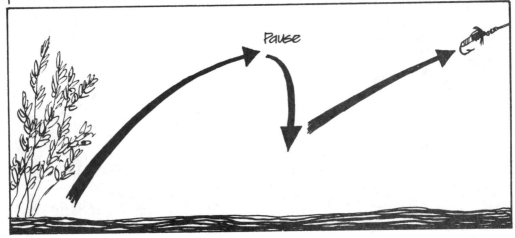

Pause

Fishing a damselfly nymph

During the early part of the season this pattern can be fished, very slowly, along the bottom. Shallower bays, where weed is prolific during the summer, are the most likely areas to attract the natural nymphs, as they feed largely on decaying vegetable matter.

During the warmer months the nymphs are far more active and wriggle to the surface, whereupon they proceed to swim towards the shore or surface weed in order to hatch into adult damselflies. To simulate this activity, fish the artificial just under the surface with a fairly fast retrieve, on a floating line.

Where there are rushes or reeds, it is often more productive to cast and retrieve along the shoreline.

Fishing a corixa

This pattern imitates the lesser water-boatman which spends most of its life near the bed of the lake, but has to rise to the surface in order to replenish its air supply.

Two patterns have developed to represent this little bug. The leaded version, which can be fished via a floating or a sinking line close to the bottom...

... and the buoyant (plastazote) version, which has to be fished with a sinking line.

Cast the buoyant corixa and allow the line to sink—the corixa will float on or near the surface.

When the line is retrieved, the corixa will dive towards the bottom, imitating, in a very life-like manner, the action of a water-boatman as it swims back to base.

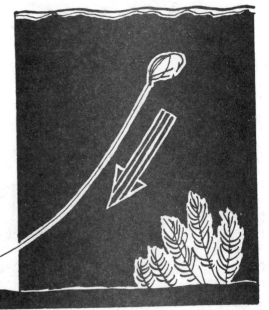

112

Fishing a leaded shrimp

This pattern represents the fresh-water shrimp, Gammarus; a resident of well-oxygenated water. They thrive in watercress, suggesting therefore that lakes fed by streams containing this plant would be ideal places to use this very effective little pattern.

The combination of lead wire and the shape of the body results in the artificial adopting an inverted attitude, which simulates the natural in a very life-like manner.

A leaded shrimp is ideally suited for margin fishing in clear-water lakes. Let the shrimp sink to the bottom where trout are patrolling.

When a trout approaches, inch the shrimp off the bottom in short jerks.

Midday: June, July and August

Bright, sunny midsummer days are not conducive to good fishing; local anglers, having fished early in the morning, take a siesta until the sun begins to drop westward. For the visiting angler who has limited time, it's Hobson's Choice. However, he should not be disheartened, because although the surface of the lake may look dead, there are areas in the deeper water which hold concentrations of fish.

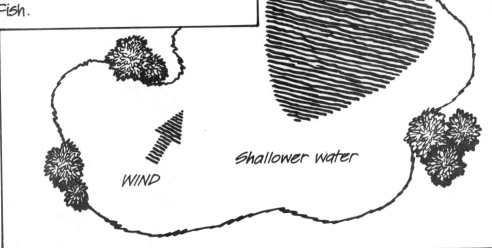

Best bank for left-handed angler.

WIND

Best bank for right-handed angler.

If the lake is man-made, the dam end is always a good place to try, especially if the wind is blowing in that direction.

A lure or large nymph on a 9ft (2·75m) leader to a No. 7-8 weight-forward or shooting-head line should make contact with deep-swimming trout.

Trout will be found very close to reservoir dams, but the fly should never be allowed to make contact with the stone or concrete structure, as this may damage the hook point.

Trout will often take a lure as it sinks, therefore positive contact should be maintained from the moment the line hits the water.

Search different depths until the fish are located

If, after a while there is no response, tie on a dropper and fish two lures.

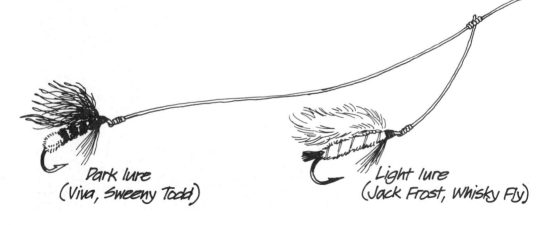

Dark lure
(Viva, Sweeny Todd)

Light lure
(Jack Frost, Whisky Fly)

Variations in retrieve can also mean the difference between success and failure.

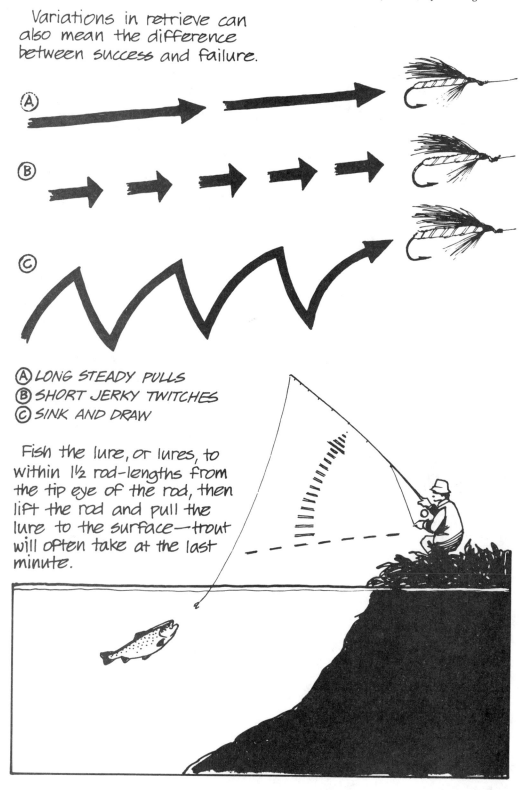

Ⓐ LONG STEADY PULLS
Ⓑ SHORT JERKY TWITCHES
Ⓒ SINK AND DRAW

Fish the lure, or lures, to within 1½ rod-lengths from the tip eye of the rod, then lift the rod and pull the lure to the surface—trout will often take at the last minute.

Lures

Ace of Spades

Appetizer

Missionary

Jack Frost

Muddler Minnow

Church Fry

Baby Doll

Polystickle

Sweeny Todd

Whisky Fly

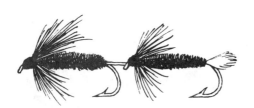

Worm Fly

Black and Orange Marabou

Badger Lure

Black Lure

Dog Nobbler

Jersey Herd

Perch Fry

Undertaker

Matuka

Viva

September and October

Autumn provides two high-lights in the year. Where coarse fish are present, the fry of roach, perch or bream form large shoals, which are continually harassed by marauding trout. Craneflies or daddy longlegs are also in abundance and often blown on to the water, where they are quickly devoured by the trout.

FRY—IMITATING LURES

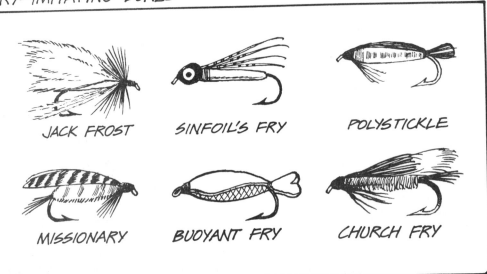

JACK FROST   SINFOIL'S FRY   POLYSTICKLE

MISSIONARY   BUOYANT FRY   CHURCH FRY

The presence of a fry-feeding trout is usually manifested by a disturbance on the surface of the water as the fry attempt to escape the lunges of the predator.

When fry-feeding trout have been located it is usually just a matter of casting, with a floating or neutral density line, into the area of activity.

VARIOUS WAYS TO PRESENT A FRY LURE

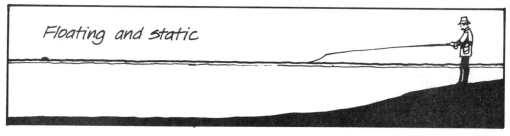

Floating and static

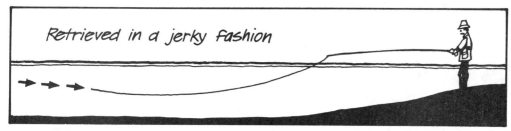

Retrieved in a jerky fashion

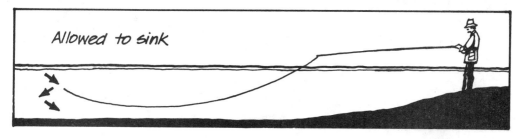

Allowed to sink

The boat angler fishing over deep water will stand more chance of contacting the bigger fry-feeding trout.

Run of the mill stock fish up to 2lb (0·90kg) chasing shoals of fry.

Ultra fast sinking or lead-core line presents lure in big fish area.

Large trout (often browns) wait for easy pickings as wounded and dead fry sink to the bottom.

MISSIONARY (an ideal lure for this method)

Fishing the daddy

Dapping with a natural daddy longlegs (cranefly) has been practised for many years on some Irish and Scottish lochs. Given the right conditions, this form of fishing can be applied to most stillwater fisheries. There is no need to use the natural insect, either — an artificial 'daddy' works just as well.

WIND

Length of floss line tied to 6lb (2·70 kg) main line.

6ft (1·85 m) leader B.S. 6lb (2·70 kg)

Fishing an artificial daddy longlegs from the bank, with a weight-forward or double-taper line, can be very effective in breezy conditions.

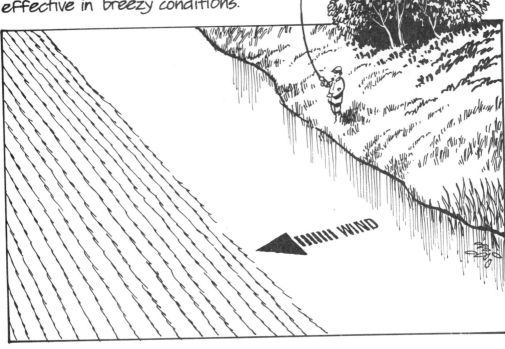

Trout will take a dry daddy longlegs if it is fished static in the surface film, but they seem to respond in a more positive manner to a fly which is dragged across the water surface.

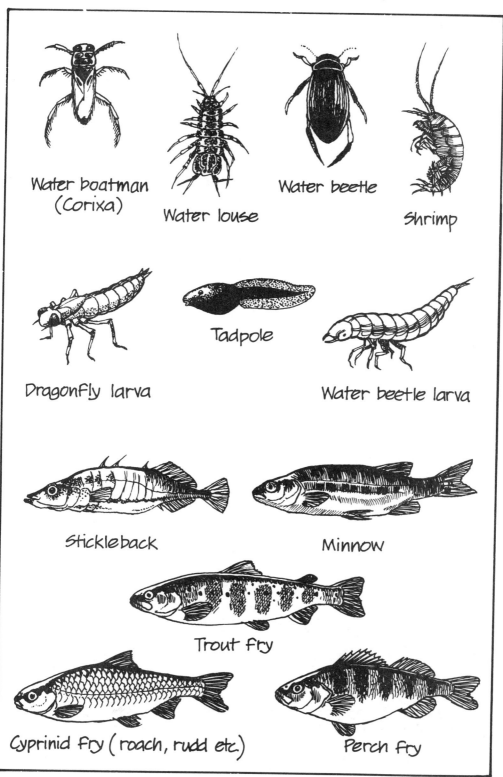

Water boatman
(Corixa)

Water louse

Water beetle

Shrimp

Dragonfly larva

Tadpole

Water beetle larva

Stickleback

Minnow

Trout fry

Cyprinid fry (roach, rudd etc.)

Perch fry

Playing and landing a stillwater trout

1

As soon as a trout is hooked, hold the rod well up.

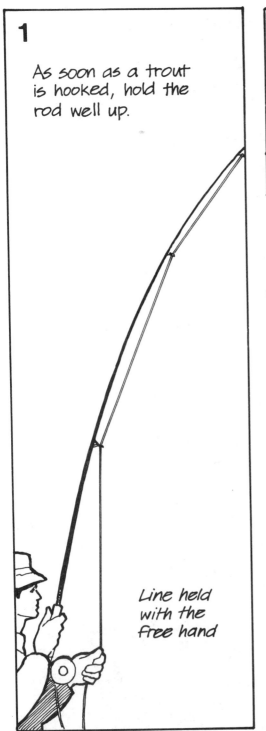

Line held with the free hand

2

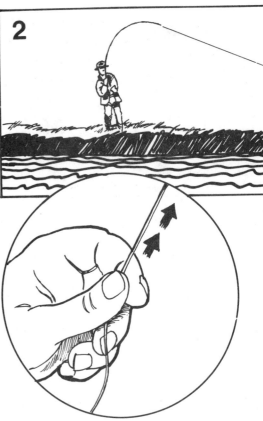

.... by letting the line slip, under pressure, through the index finger and thumb.

4

The fish can now be played from the reel.

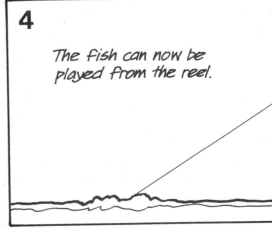

When a trout feels the resistance of the rod and line it will often take off on a powerful run, and should be given its head....

3

At this point, a few backward steps should get rid of any loose coils of line which may have been lying on the bank.

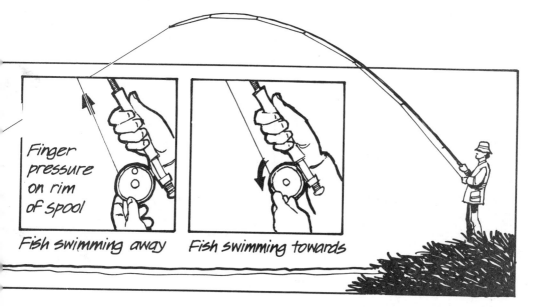

Finger pressure on rim of spool

Fish swimming away

Fish swimming towards

Many anglers play a fish directly from the line, and while this is fine up to a point, and very efficient for keeping in touch with a trout which is swimming rapidly towards the angler, there is the problem of having loose coils of line lying on the bank which could become snagged or tangled and result in a lost fish.

The best way to turn a trout away from snags is to apply side strain.

When a trout is ready for the net it will tend to keel over on its side.

Draw the fish over the frame of the stationary net. NEVER jab at the fish in an attempt to scoop it out.

Lift the frame clear of the water, draw the net towards the bank and lift, stepping back at the same time. The last three movements should be done in one smooth easy action. Large trout will probably have to be dragged up the bank.

Accessories

LANDING NET: For river and small stream fishing where the angler is constantly on the move, and often up to his knees in water, a collapsible short-handled net is convenient. When fishing a lake the long-handled version is more practical.

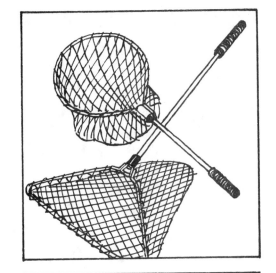

WAISTCOAT: This is a valuable piece of clothing which enables small, but important bits of equipment to be carried close to hand.

HAT: It is always advisable to wear a hat, especially when fishing a lake where long casts are often necessary ; it provides protection as well as shading the eyes.

BINOCULARS: A scan of the water surface with binoculars will often reveal the presence of feeding fish. They are also very useful for insect spotting.

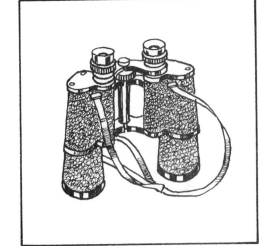

Accessories

SCISSORS: A good quality, sharp pair of scissors are essential for trimming knot ends or clipping unwanted hackle from flies. For safety's sake, stick the points into a cork.

BASS BAG: These bags are sold at many stillwater fisheries, and are the ideal container for retaining your catch and keeping it fresh.

FLY WALLET

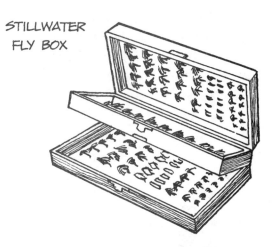

FLY BOX

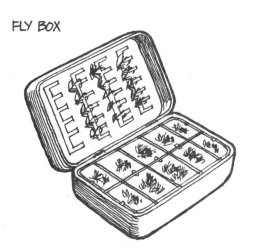

STILLWATER
FLY BOX

Accessories

LINE TRAY: The ideal receptacle for storing loose line during the retrieve. The alternative is to let the line fall to the ground, where it may become snagged in bank-side undergrowth. Most anglers, however, prefer to fish without a line tray.

PRIEST: The most humane way of dispatching a trout is to deal it one or two blows on the head with this impliment. Some priests are equipped with a marrow scoop. By inserting the scoop through the mouth and into the stomach of the dead trout a sample of the stomach contents can be withdrawn. A survey will quickly reveal on what insects the trout has been feeding.

Stag Horn Priest

Marrow Scoop / Priest

POLAROID GLASSES: These are in-valuable for cutting out glare from the water surface. For stalking clear-water trout they are perfect, as they enable the angler to see into the water.

Knots

BLOOD KNOT: For joining lengths of different breaking strain nylon in order to produce a tapered leader. Recommended breaking strains are shown in another section of this book.

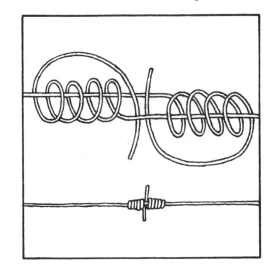

TUCKED HALF-BLOOD KNOT: Unlike the basic half-blood knot, this knot will not slip, and is the ideal knot for connecting a fly to the point or dropper of a leader.

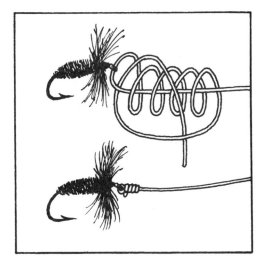

DROPPER KNOT: There is more than one knot can be used for this purpose. The water knot shown, however, permits the use of nylon equal in breaking strain to that of the point to be connected further up, where the main leader is thicker.

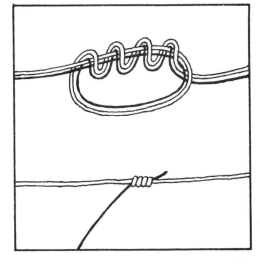

Knots

Here are three more knots which can be used to secure a fly to a leader. These knots are more suited to small dry flies — use the tucked half blood knot for larger hooks.

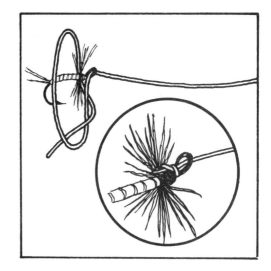

HALF HITCH

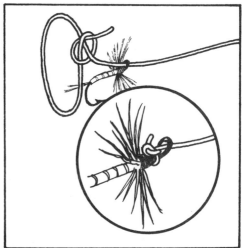

TURLE KNOT

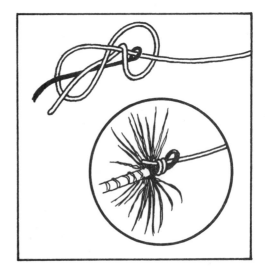

WOOD KNOT

How to cure a loose ferrule

Spigot ferrules, especially those on carbon fibre rods, tend to wear loose very quickly.

Spigot ferrule

A loose ferrule can be noticed immediately, because the male and female sections are touching one another when the rod is assembled.

To produce a tighter fit, rub the male section with candle wax.

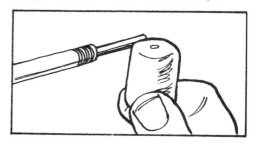

If the ferrule is very badly worn, more drastic measures will have to be taken.

Cut about ¼ in (6 mm) from the female section, then re-whip to provide support.

A correctly fitting spigot ferrule should look like this.

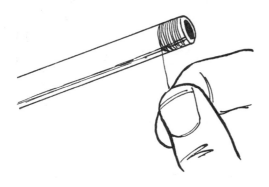

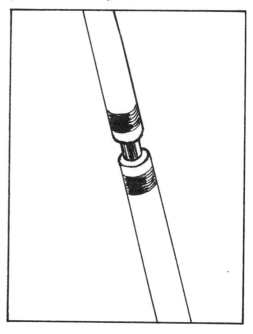

Whipping on a ring

Rods can be purchased in a half completed state, with just the handle and reel fitting secured to the blank. The rings are left to the angler. Ring positioning information is provided with the rod.

Start by securing one side of each ring to the rod. Sellotape is the ideal material for this.

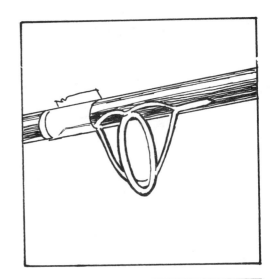

If single leg fuji rings are being used, a drop of super-glue will keep them in position, ready for whipping. Now is the time to make sure that all the rings are exactly in line.

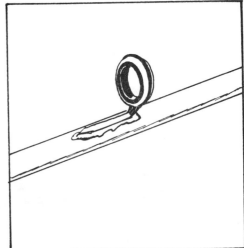

Starting at a point on the rod, just clear of the foot of the ring, wind the whipping thread back on itself for five or six turns, and cut off the tag end.

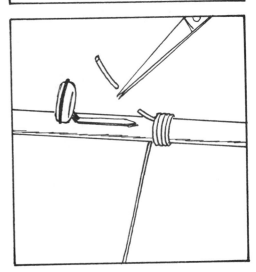

Whipping on a ring

Continue whipping, making sure that the turns are tight to one another. About five turns short of where you intend to finish, insert a loop of whipping thread or nylon monofilament, and continue whipping over this loop.

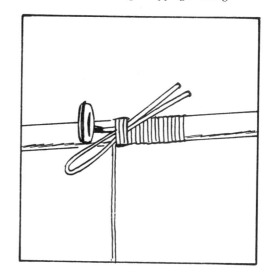

Making sure that a steady tension is being maintained, push the end of the whipping through the eye of the loop.

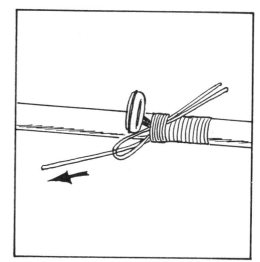

Pull the loop through the whipping, and keep pulling until the end of the whipping is completely through. Cut off the tag end.

If the ring has two feet, repeat the whole operation, after removing the sellotape. When all the rings are secured coat the whippings with two or three layers of varnish.

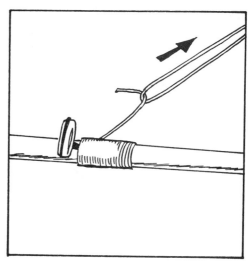

Licence

SOUTH WEST WATER AUTHORITY   **ROD LICENCE**   4704

Licencee's Full Name
(BLOCK LETTERS)   Mr. R. HOWARD

Permanent Address   CLEAVE COTTAGE
(BLOCK LETTERS)
                         OAKFORD   TS1

Date of Issue 3/5/84   Time of issue 11-15

                         LINESPORTS

Distributor

1984   TROUT ANNUAL   £5·60

It is most important that, before you go rushing off to the nearest river to catch a trout, you are in possession of a trout rod licence. Permission is also needed from the riparian owner of the land through which the river flows. If an angling club controls the fishing rights, a permit issued by that club will be required.

Many private and water authority stillwater fisheries issue block permits which include, in the fee, the charge for a rod licence.

A trout licence entitles the licensee to fish for coarse fish and trout, but not salmon or sea trout. Salmon parr accidently caught while trout fishing should be returned to the water.

How to identify a salmon parr.

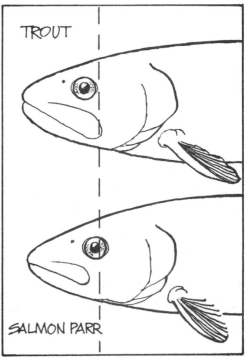

TROUT

SALMON PARR

Introduction to fly-tying

I am constantly amazed by the fact that such noble fish as the trout and salmon can be caught on such unlikely creations of fur and feather as those we anglers often cobble together and call a fly – whether it be an imitation of some natural insect or a flashy attractor fly that serves to arouse the fish's predatory or territorial instincts. Such is the enjoyment found in tying and fishing the fly that often the angler becomes as firmly hooked on the sport as the fish on the fly!

True success as an angler cannot be bought, and this applies in particular to the business of becoming a successful fly fisherman or woman. The most expensive and perfect fly rod and tackle in the world cannot cover up deficiencies in a person's casting technique. A wallet of the most perfectly tied flies will assure some degree of success – if properly finished – but almost all fly patterns have a regional or seasonal variation, often of a most subtle kind. Such regional or seasonal variations are an intelligent response to conditions peculiar to that particular fishery or environment. The only way an angler can obtain flies that fit a particular need (and the angler's subjective preferences) is for the angler to tie those flies with that need in the mind.

Tony Whieldon has drawn this section, almost it must be said, from the heart. His first love is flyfishing but it is his strongly held view that no one can consider themselves a true flyfisher until an apprenticeship has been served at a fly-tying vice.

It is through his artist's eye and skilled interpretation, his observation of detail and, when he ties flies, the almost simplistic representation of insect life which he created at his vice, that his true skill becomes evident in recognising those features which a fish expects to see in nature. This is perhaps one of the most difficult angling skills to acquire, but one essential to anyone who would aspire to success.

There are some who believe in the exact imitation, or as close as can be achieved within the limitations of the flydresser's art. Their insect imitations are wondrously close to the real thing and are marvels of the fly-tyers' art and skill.

But there has always been another argument. All too often the water is cloudy. The water itself can give rise to an inherent optical distortion; light and shadow and the time of day affect the appearance of objects in the water. So it is a widely held view that the exact imitation is not always the best deceiver of fish.

Tony's view in this argument is that rather than let these nuances of light and shadow defeat the object, they should be used to enhance the allure of the fly. The silhouette should be correct, but not sharply defined. Where there is a shiny surface in nature, use a material which will reflect or sparkle. Colours should be representative rather than faithfully duplicated, especially as different materials may not transmit the same colour as the original (one reason, incidentally, to follow a traditional pattern material that has been found to work).

Most important of all, the fly should be fished in the right place and at the right time. This feel for what is right – almost an extra-sensory perception possessed by some anglers as to where the fish will be and what they will be feeding on – is a perception developed through being prepared to listen to what others have to say through observation and an understanding of the living world around us.

This sense of accord and observation is far more important than the precise execution of a fly-tying recipe. However, natural proportion, symmetry and movement should exert their influence not only in the tying of the fly, but also in its presentation to the fish.

As I have already said, Tony's skill as a flyfisherman is matched by his artistic ability. Blended with a rounded mixture of commonsense and practical ability, these skills are reflected in this section, ensuring that it contains all that is really necessary to tie flies which are effective fish catchers. Beyond this, practice will make perfect – or so we like to think!

Russell Symons,
Plymouth, Devon.

Tools

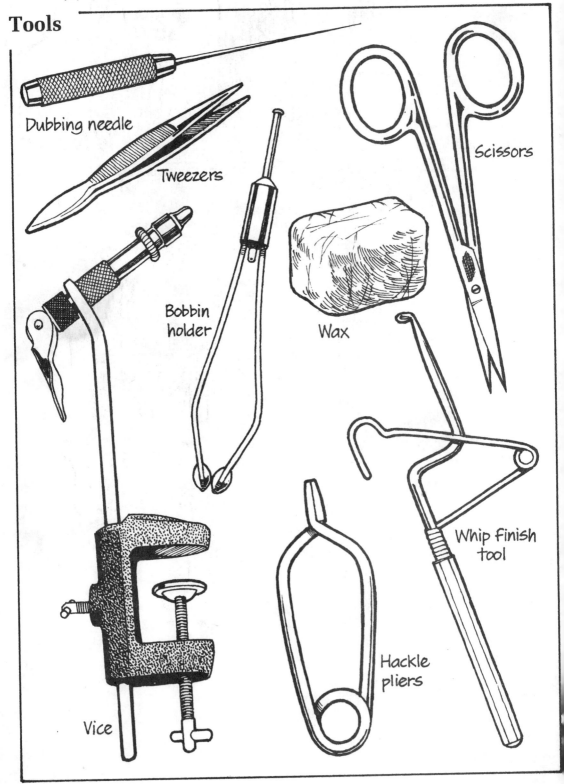

Dubbing needle

Tweezers

Scissors

Bobbin holder

Wax

Vice

Hackle pliers

Whip finish tool

Hooks

Sproat hooks with a turned-down eye are ideal for winged and hackled wet flies, and for certain short-bodied nymphs.

Fine wire hooks with a turned-up eye are best for dry flies.

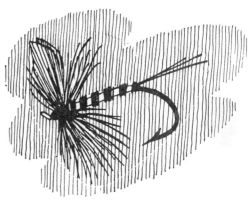

Long-shank hooks with a turned-down eye are used for dressing lures and nymphs.

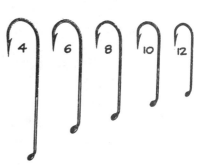

143

Materials

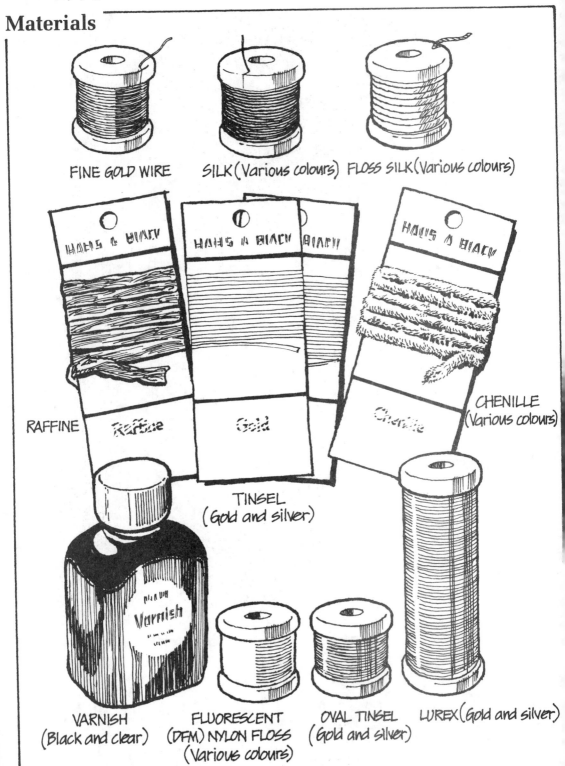

FINE GOLD WIRE

SILK (Various colours)

FLOSS SILK (Various colours)

RAFFINE

TINSEL
(Gold and silver)

CHENILLE
(Various colours)

VARNISH
(Black and clear)

FLUORESCENT
(DFM) NYLON FLOSS
(Various colours)

OVAL TINSEL
(Gold and silver)

LUREX (Gold and silver)

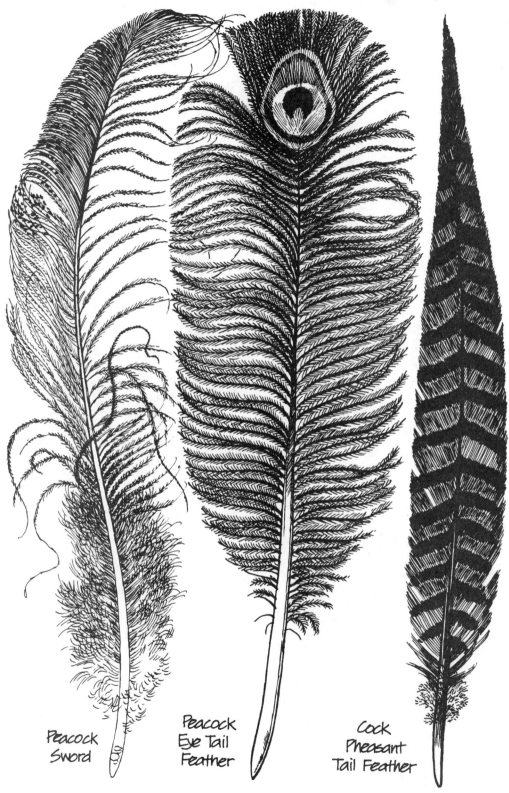

Peacock
Sword

Peacock
Eye Tail
Feather

Cock
Pheasant
Tail Feather

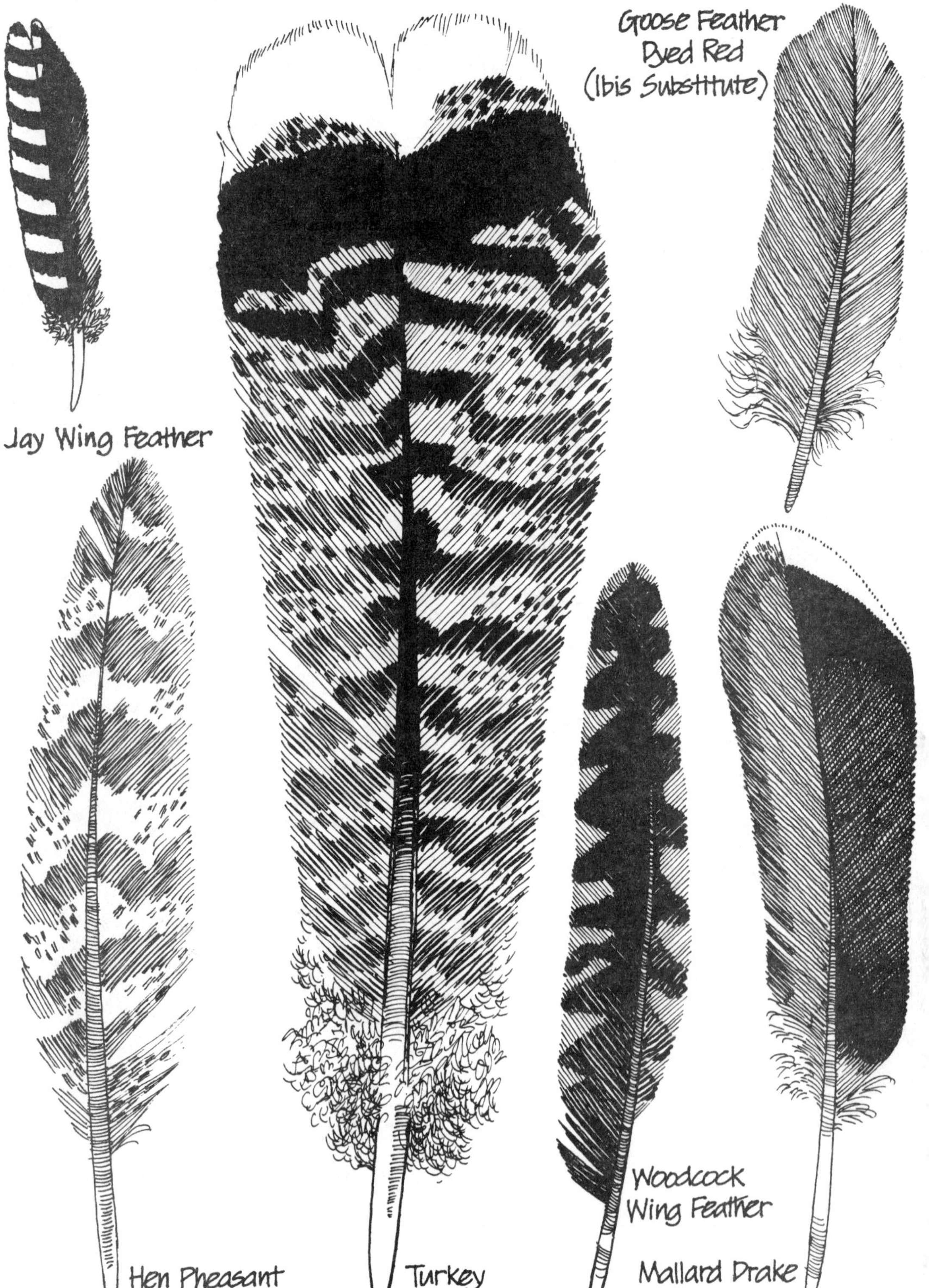

Goose Feather
Dyed Red
(Ibis Substitute)

Jay Wing Feather

Hen Pheasant
Wing Feather

Turkey
Tail Feather

Woodcock
Wing Feather

Mallard Drake
Wing Feather

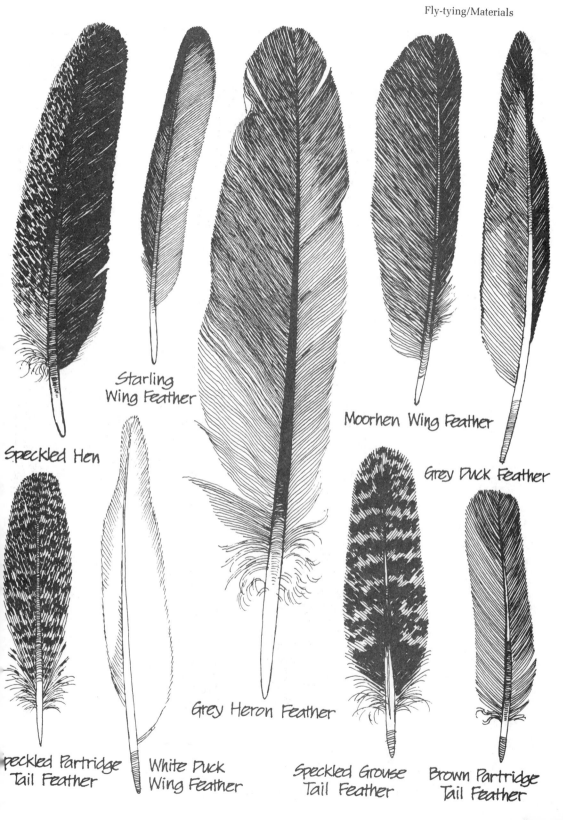

Starling Wing Feather

Moorhen Wing Feather

Grey Duck Feather

Speckled Hen

Grey Heron Feather

peckled Partridge Tail Feather

White Duck Wing Feather

Speckled Grouse Tail Feather

Brown Partridge Tail Feather

Cock hackles are best bought on the cape. The cape shown below is an actual size badger variation. The long-fibred hackles at the tip provide tail fibres for aquatic fly imitations and wings for lures (streamer flies). The middle region of the cape provides hackles for medium-size dry flies, while the small hackles at the base are ideal for dry flies tied to very small hooks. Saddle hackles, from the back of the cockerel, come individually and provide wings for large lures.

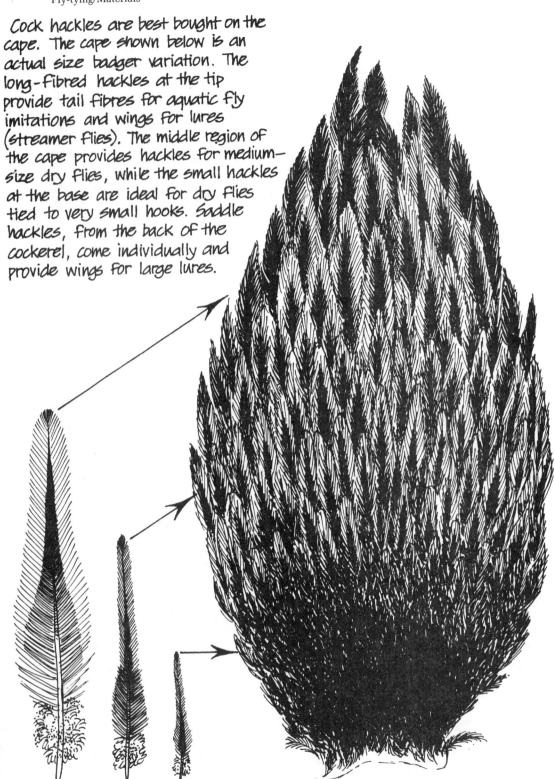

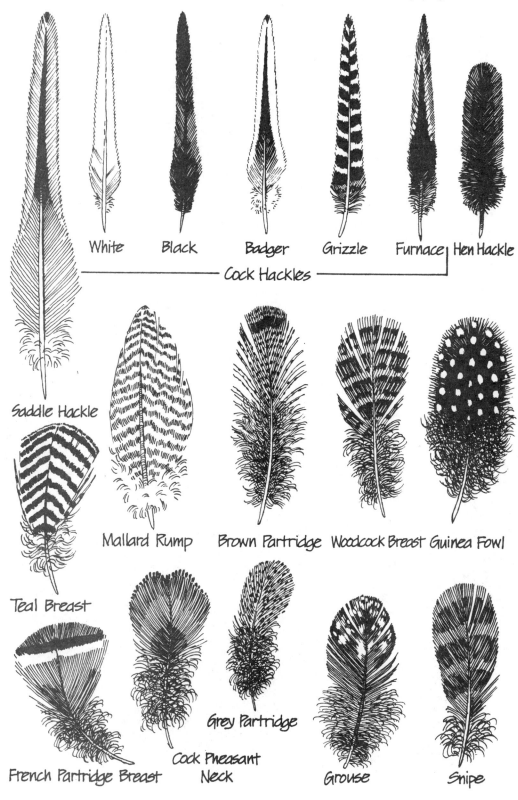

White · Black · Badger · Grizzle · Furnace | Hen Hackle

Cock Hackles

Saddle Hackle

Teal Breast

Mallard Rump · Brown Partridge · Woodcock Breast · Guinea Fowl

French Partridge Breast

Cock Pheasant Neck

Grey Partridge

Grouse

Snipe

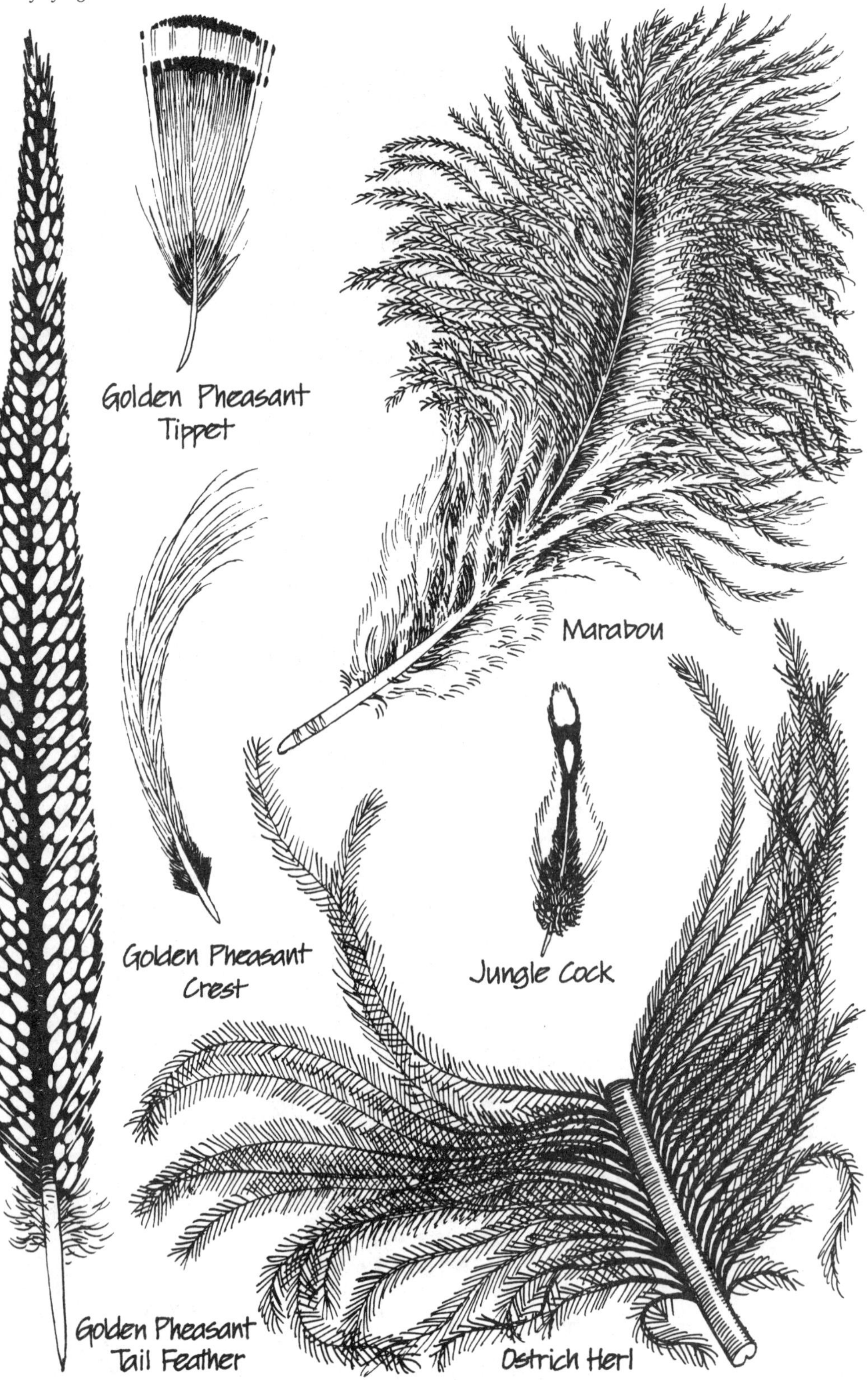

Golden Pheasant
Tippet

Marabou

Golden Pheasant
Crest

Jungle Cock

Golden Pheasant
Tail Feather

Ostrich Herl

Stoat Tail

Black Squirrel Tail   Grey Squirrel Tail   Hare's Ear

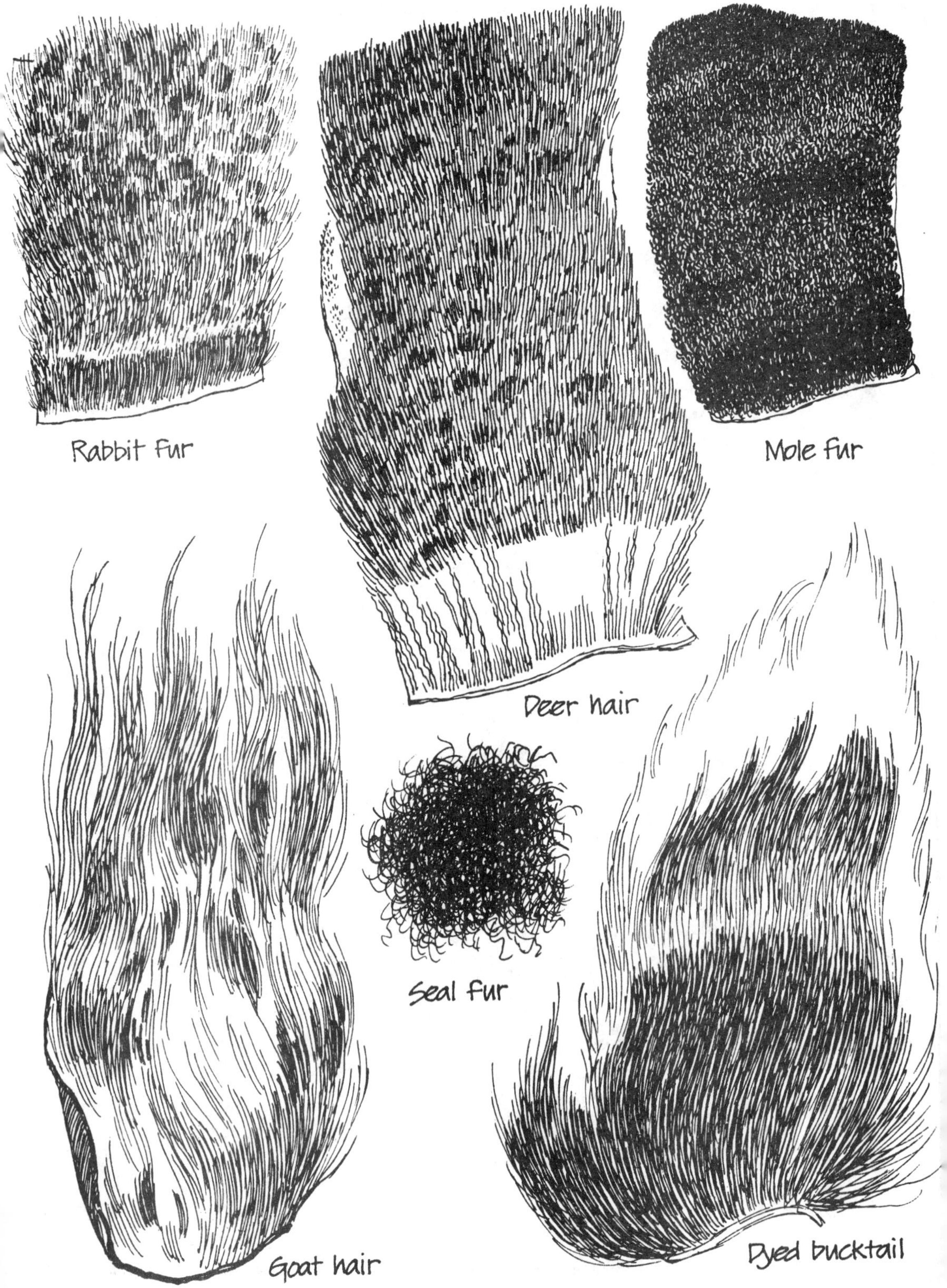

Rabbit fur

Mole fur

Deer hair

Goat hair

Seal fur

Dyed bucktail

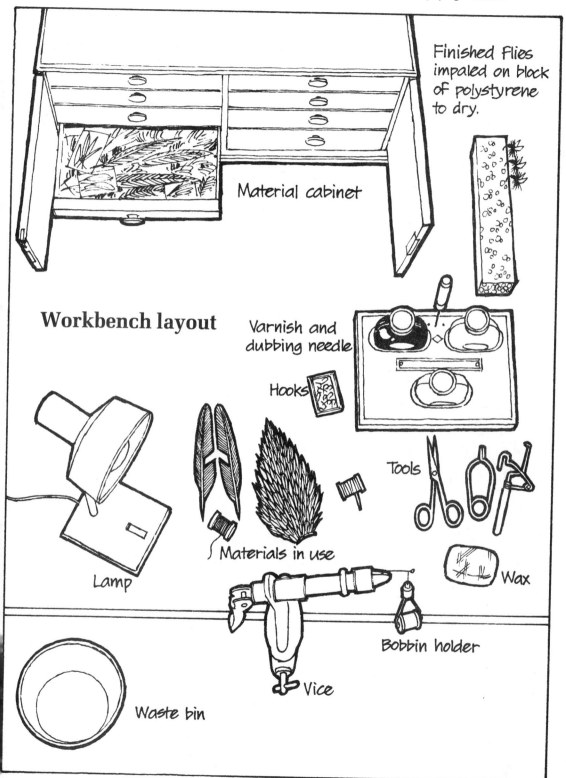

Finished Flies impaled on block of polystyrene to dry.

Material cabinet

Workbench layout

Varnish and dubbing needle

Hooks

Tools

Materials in use

Lamp

Wax

Bobbin holder

Vice

Waste bin

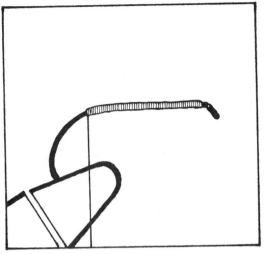

Dubbing a body

Materials for dubbing a body include mole fur, rabbit and hare fur, seal's fur, as well as synthetic fibres in various colours.

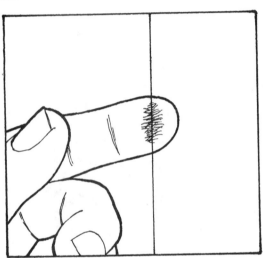

Wind a layer of well waxed silk along the shank of the hook. Apply a further rubbing of wax to the silk hanging between the hook and the bobbin.

Pinch out a very small amount of the required material, between finger and thumb, and place it against the silk. Pinch the material using an even pressure and rotate the dubbing and silk in one direction only. Release finger pressure and repeat the process until the dubbing is left hanging on the silk.

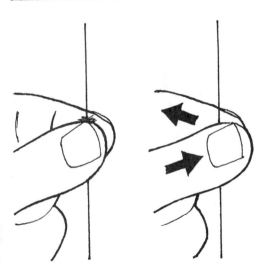

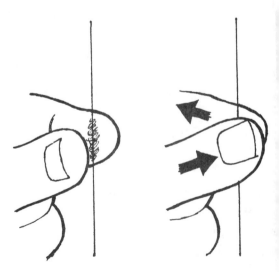

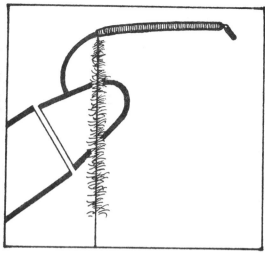

Further spinnings will eventually result in a length of dubbed silk which can be wound up the shank of the hook.

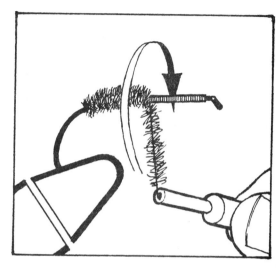

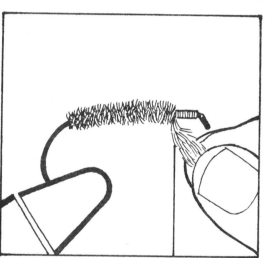

When the required length of dubbing has been wound on to the shank, any excess material left on the hanging silk can be pulled away. The rest of the fly can then be completed in the normal manner.

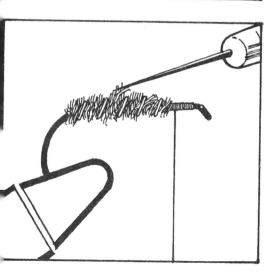

Where a rib material features in a dressing, which it does in most cases, the dubbing tends to flatten a little as the rib is wound over it. The dubbing can be revived by teasing the strands with a dubbing needle.

Making a whip finish (by hand)

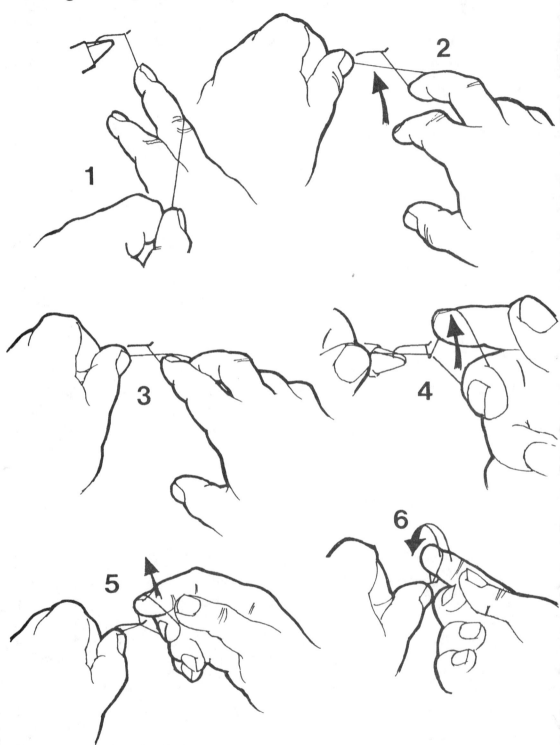

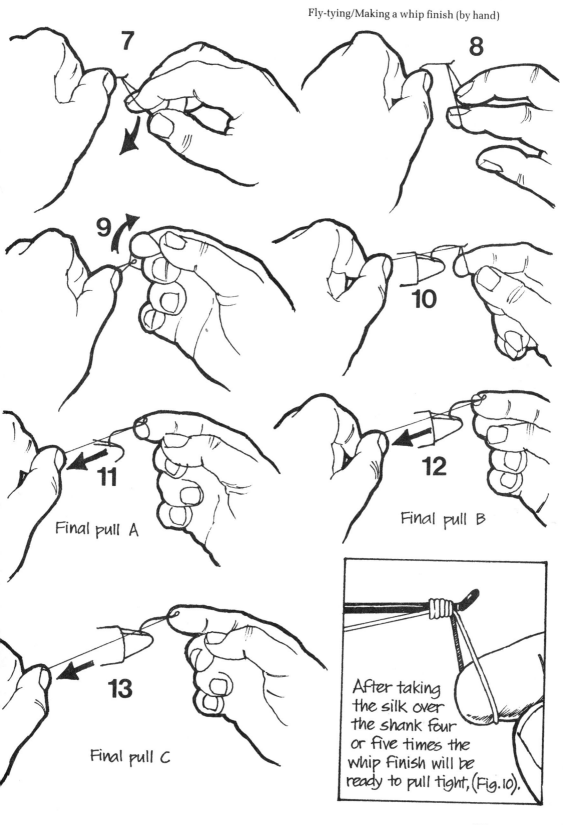

7

8

9

10

Final pull A

11

12

Final pull B

Final pull C

13

After taking the silk over the shank four or five times the whip finish will be ready to pull tight, (Fig. 10).

Making a whip finish (with a tool)

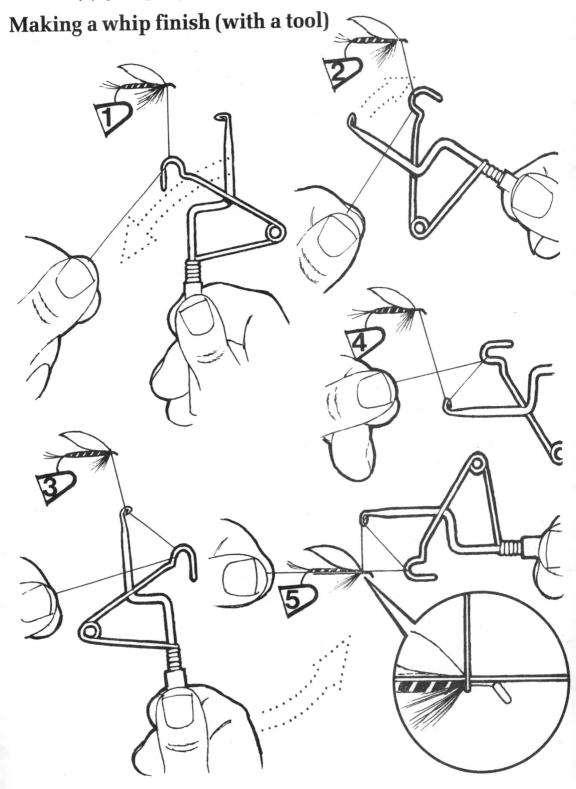

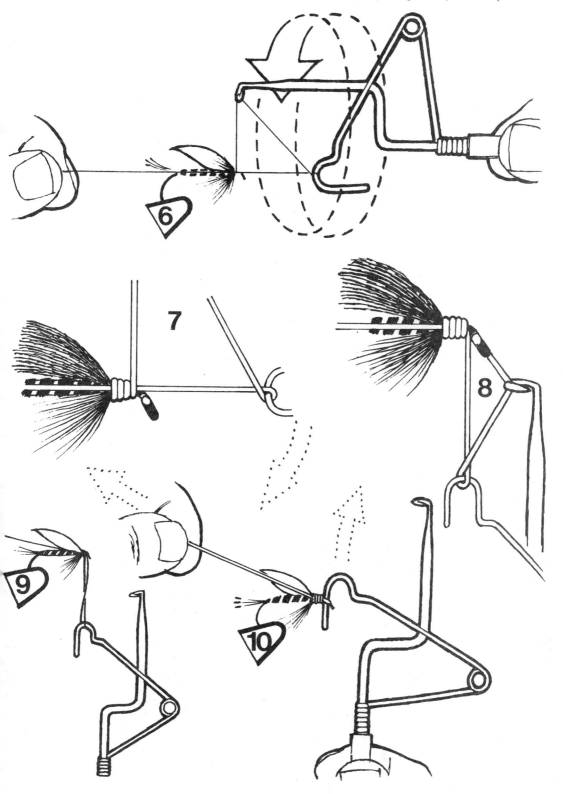

Tying a hackled dry fly

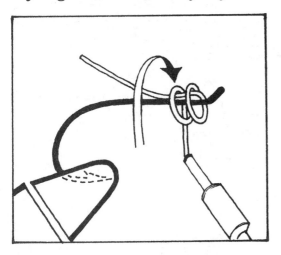

Place a fine-wire up-eyed hook in the vice. The point of the hook should be hidden to prevent it snagging on the tying silk.

Using well-waxed tying silk, wind a neat layer along the shank of the hook. The leading end can be trapped, as shown, and the tag trimmed off before proceeding.

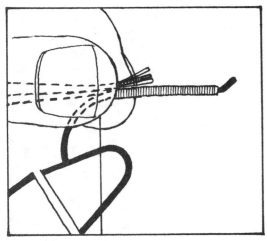

Select a few fibres from a cock hackle (the longer hackles in the cape are best for tails), and tie them in at the bend.

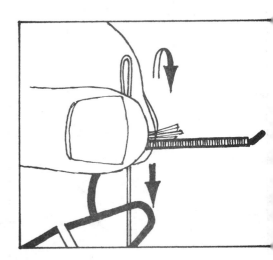

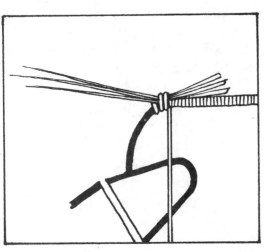

Pinch and loop the silk two or three times over the tail to clamp it to the top of the hook. One turn of silk under the tail will give it a nice cock.

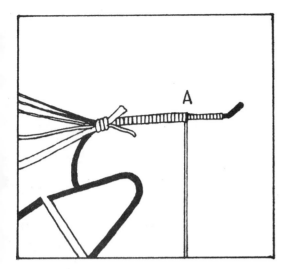

Now trap a length of body material and ribbing. Body materials vary widely, but in this instance we will assume that the fly has a body of floss silk, and a ribbing of gold wire.

After securing the components of the body, wind the silk back to the point where the body is to finish.

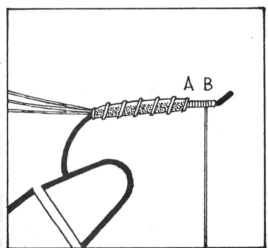

The body floss is now wound on and secured with the tying silk at point 'A'. The ribbing is then wound along the body in neat, even spirals. This also is secured with the tying silk at point 'A'. Excess body and rib material is trimmed off and the tying silk is taken to point 'B'.

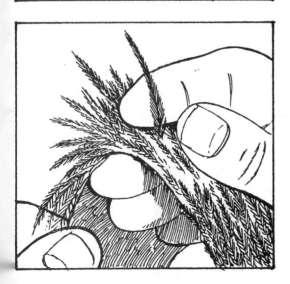

Select a suitable hackle from the cape. This can best be done by bending the cape at the desired spot which will cause the hackles to stand up, making selection a lot easier. The length of the hackle fibre needs to be about one and a half times the gape of the hook.

Tying a hackled dry fly (cont.)

Soft, fluffy fibres near the base of the hackle quill should be pulled off. The prepared hackle should now look like this.

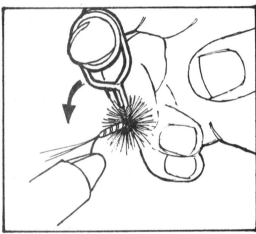

Hold the hackle alongside the hook shank and trap the quill with two or three turns of tying silk, then pull the hackle to a position at right angles to the shank. Continue winding the tying silk, immediately behind the quill, up to the body. The hackle should now be held in a fixed position by tightly butted silk on either side. The concave bias of the hackle should face forwards.

Grip the hackle point with hackle pliers and carefully wind the hackle towards the body, where it should be trapped with two turns of silk.

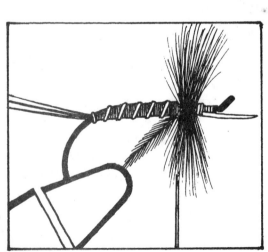

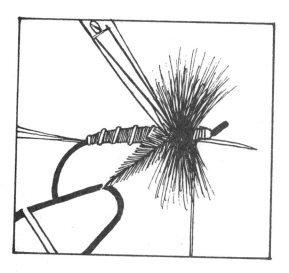

Carefully ease the tying silk back through the hackle, trapping the hackle quill in the process. Snip off the unwanted hackle tip and the excess quill. Trimming with a sharp pair of fly-tying scissors should be done with the utmost care, making sure that the points are clear of the tying silk.

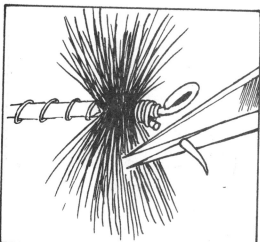

Once the quill has been cut away, the head can be built up and the cut quill-end hidden from view. While this is being done it is best to hold the hackle back, out of the way.

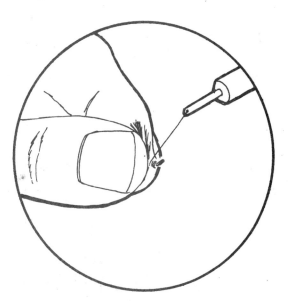

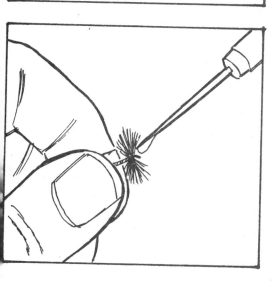

All that remains now is to tie in a whip finish, trim off the tying silk and treat the head of the fly with a drop of clear varnish.

Hackled dry fly dressings

PHEASANT TAIL
Hook | 10-14.
Tying silk | Brown.
Body | Cock pheasant tail fibres, ribbed with gold wire.
Hackle | Golden dun cock.
Tail | Golden dun cock hackle fibres.

COCH-Y-BONDDU
Hook | 12-14.
Tying silk | Brown.
Body | Two or three strands of peacock herl, with fine flat gold tinsel tip.
Hackle | Furnace cock.

IRON BLUE DUN
Hook | 12-14.
Tying silk | Red.
Tail | Iron blue cock hackle fibres.
Body | Mole fur dubbing with a red butt.
Hackle | Iron blue cock.

GREY DUSTER
Hook | 10-14.
Tying silk | Brown.
Body | Dubbing of light rabbit's fur mixed with a small amount of blue under-fur.
Hackle | Badger cock with a good dark centre.

TUP'S INDISPENSABLE
Hook | 14-16.
Tying silk | Yellow.
Body | Rear end- Yellow floss or tying silk. Remainder- pinkish lamb's wool.
Hackle | Honey cock.
Tail | Honey cock hackle fibres.

BLUE UPRIGHT
Hook | 10-14.
Tying silk | Purple.
Body | Well marked stripped peacock quill.
Hackle | Medium blue dun cock.
Tail | Medium blue dun cock fibres.

RED SPINNER
Hook   12-14.
Tying silk Brown.
Tail   Red cock hackle Fibres.
Body ·   Red Floss, ribbed with fine
          Flat gold tinsel.
Hackle   Rear- Red cock.
          Front- Blue dun cock.

GINGER QUILL
Hook   14-16.
Tying silk Orange.
Tail   Ginger cock hackle Fibres.
Body   Stripped peacock quill.
Hackle   Ginger cock.

MARCH BROWN
Hook   10-14.
Tying silk Yellow.
Tail   Brown partridge Fibres.
Body   Hare's fur spun thinly.
Hackle   Rear- Dun cock.
          Front- Brown partridge back
          feather.

RED TAG
Hook   12-14.
Tying silk Brown.
Tag   Bright red wool or red floss.
Body   Bronze green peacock herl.
Hackle   Red cock.

CINNAMON QUILL
Hook   12-14.
Tying silk Brown.
Tail   Ginger cock hackle Fibres.
Body   Stripped peacock herl.
Hackle   Ginger cock.

DOUBLE BADGER
Hook   12-14.
Tying silk Black.
Body   Three strands of peacock
          herl.
Hackle   Badger cock — one at the
          head and one at the tail.

Tying an upright-winged dry fly

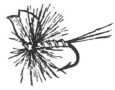

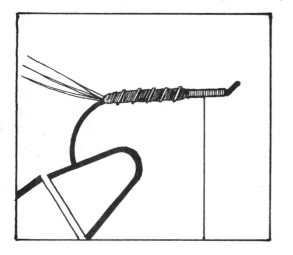

Place a fine-wire hook in the vice and proceed exactly as with a hackled dry fly up to the point where the body has been completed.

It is purely a matter of choice whether an up-eyed or down-eyed hook is used. The former looks prettier, but I doubt very much that the trout has such aesthetic discrimination.

The wings are cut from a pair of matching left and right wing feathers.

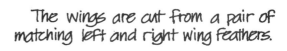

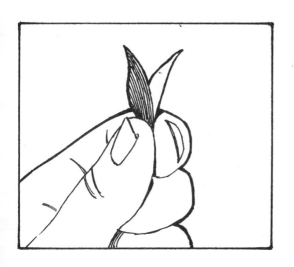

When placed together the wing slips should have the concave faces pointing outwards. Handle the slips very gingerly at this stage, as they have a tendency to break up. If this does occur, cut a new set.

To minimize the risk of this happening grip the slips firmly; try to avoid a sliding movement between finger and thumb.

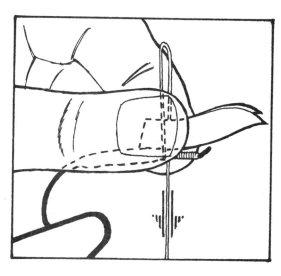

Pinch the slips together between the forefinger and thumb and hold them on the hook shank. Form a long loop over the slips, between finger and thumb, and pull down to trap the wings against the hook shank. Three turns of silk should be enough to hold the slips in place. Check that the slips are sitting squarely along the hook shank.

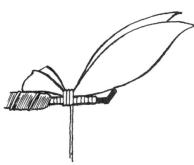

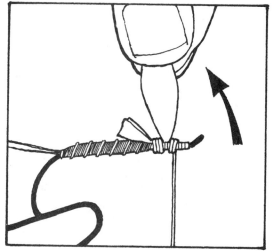

Move the finger and thumb to the tip of the slips and lift them upright. Make a couple of turns of silk tight against the front edge of the slips to trap them in an upright position.

Take one turn of silk around the base of the wing slips.

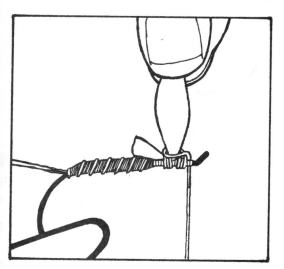

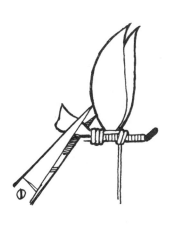

Trim off any excess wing material.

Tying an upright-winged dry fly (cont.)

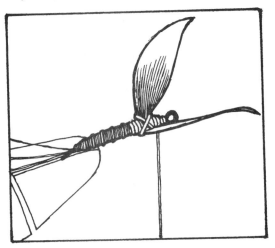

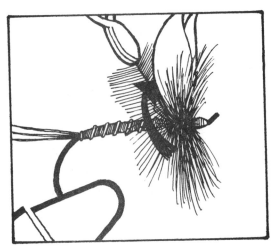

Now make a cross-over of silk between the wings, easing them apart a little more.

Select a good quality cock hackle and tie on, using the same procedure as in the tying of the hackled dry fly. Wind the hackle carefully around the shank, first in front of the wings, then to the rear. Trap the end of the hackle with tying silk and then bring the silk back through the hackle, making sure that the wings are not disfigured in the process.

Trim off the waste hackle point and quill, build up a neat head, whip finish and trim off the silk. Coat the head with clear varnish.

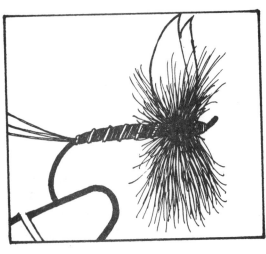

Winged dry fly dressings

COACHMAN
Hook   10-16.
Silk   Brown.
Body   Bronze peacock herl.
Wings   From a white duck wing.
Hackle Natural red cock.

RED QUILL
Hook   14-16.
Silk   Red.
Body   Stripped peacock herl.
Wings   From a starling wing.
Hackle and tail Red cock.

FLIGHT'S FANCY
Hook   12-16.
Silk   Yellow.
Body   Pale yellow floss, ribbed with flat gold tinsel.
Wings   From a pale starling wing.
Hackle and tail Honeydun cock.

POPE'S NONDESCRIPT
Hook   12-16.
Silk   Crimson.
Body   Apple green floss, ribbed with flat gold tinsel.
Wings   From a starling wing.
Hackle and tail Red cock.

HARDY'S FAVOURITE
Hook   10-14.
Silk   Red.
Body   Claret floss silk, ribbed with bronze peacock herl.
Wings   From a woodcock wing.
Hackle Partridge breast feather.
Tail   Golden pheasant tippets.

GOLD-RIBBED HARE'S EAR
Hook   12-16.
Silk   Yellow.
Body   Dubbed hare's fur ribbed with flat gold tinsel.
Wings   From a pale wing feather of a starling.
Hackle Longer strands of the body picked out with a needle.

YELLOW SALLY

Hook   12–16.
Silk   Primrose.
Body   Yellow dyed seal's fur, ribbed with primrose tying silk.
Wings   From any fine light-coloured wing dyed yellow.
Hackle   Natural light ginger cock.

WICKHAM'S FANCY

Hook   12–14.
Silk   Brown.
Body   Flat gold tinsel, ribbed with fine gold wire.
Tail   Red cock fibres.
Wings   From starling or duck wing.
Hackle   Red game cock.

ROUGH OLIVE

Hook   12–14.
Silk   Brown.
Body   Heron herl dyed olive, ribbed with gold wire.
Wings   From a starling wing feather.
Hackle   Dark blue dun cock.

DRIFFIELD DUN

Hook   14–16.
Silk   Yellow.
Body   Pale blue seal's fur, ribbed with yellow tying silk.
Wings   From a pale starling feather.
Hackle   Ginger cock.

GREENWELL'S GLORY

Hook   12–14.
Silk   Yellow (well waxed).
Body   Yellow tying silk, ribbed with fine gold wire.
Wings   From a dark starling feather.
Hackle   Light furnace cock.

HOFLAND'S FANCY

Hook   12–16.
Silk   Yellow.
Body   Crimson floss with yellow tying silk butt.
Wings   From a hen pheasant wing.
Hackle   Natural red cock.

Tying a variant dry fly

Tie the wings exactly as shown for the upright-wing version, but omit the turns of silk which bring the wings to the upright position as shown in Fig. 6.

Tie the complete hackle to the rear of the wings, then bring the silk to the front of the wings, whip finish and varnish.

BADGER VARIANT
Tying silk   Red.
Body   Stripped peacock quill.
Wings   From a starling wing feather.
Hackle   Badger cock, large.

RED VARIANT
Tying silk   Red.
Body   Stripped peacock quill.
Wings   From a starling wing feather.
Hackle   Natural red cock, large.

RUSTY VARIANT
Tying silk   Red.
Body   Yellow floss.
Wings   From a partridge wing feather.
Hackle   Rusty dun cock, large.

GREENWELL'S VARIANT
Body   Waxed yellow tying silk ribbed with fine gold wire.
Wings   From a starling wing feather.
Hackle   Light furnace cock, large.

Tying a spent-wing dry fly

After tying the body, as described earlier, select two hackles of equal size. Strip away the fibres to leave the length of wing required. Cut away excess quill and whip both hackles to the hook shank.

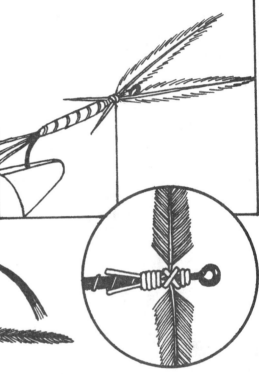

Pull each hackle back separately and lock into position as shown. Take two or three turns of silk towards the eye. This is the point where the hackle will start, and the procedure for tying that is exactly as shown for the hackled and winged dry fly.

Before tying in the hackle, snip off any excess hackle quill, especially if it is overlapping the body.

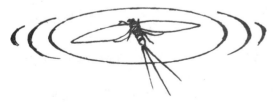

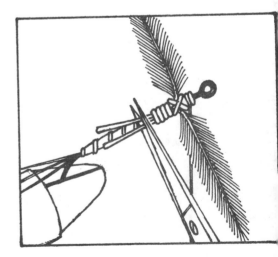

Spent-wing dry fly dressings

LUNN'S PARTICULAR
Hook	14–16.
Tying silk	Crimson.
Tail	Natural red cock hackle fibres.
Body	Natural red cock hackle stalk.
Wings	Medium blue dun cock hackle tips.
Hackle	Natural medium red cock.

HOUGHTON RUBY
Hook	14–16.
Tying silk	Crimson.
Tail	White cock hackle fibres.
Body	Hackle stalk dyed red.
Wings	Light blue dun hen. hackle tips.
Hackle	Bright Rhode Island Red cock.

WINGED YELLOW BOY
Hook	14–16.
Tying silk	Pale orange.
Tail	Pale buff hackle fibres.
Body	White hackle stalk dyed medium yellow.
Wings	Light buff cock hackle tips.
Hackle	Light buff cock.

SHERRY SPINNER
Hook	14–16
Tying silk	Pale orange.
Tail	Pale ginger hackle fibres.
Body	Orange floss silk ribbed with fine gold wire.
Wings	Light blue dun hen hackle tips.
Hackle	Rhode Island Red cock.

Mayfly dressings

SPENT GNAT
Tail   Three fibres from a cock pheasant tail.
Body   White translucent plastic.
Wings   Dark blue hackle points.
Hackle   Badger cock.

YELLOW PARTRIDGE HACKLE
Tail   Three fibres from a cock pheasant tail.
Body   White floss silk.
Rear hackle   Yellow cock.
Front hackle   Grey partridge.

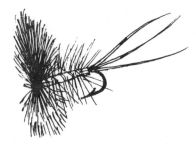

HACKLE FIBRE WING
Tail   Three fibres from a cock pheasant tail.
Body   Natural raffia, ribbed with silver oval tinsel.
Body hackle   Medium olive cock.
Wings   Fibres of large honey dun cock hackle dyed olive, and tied upright.
Shoulder hackle   Badger cock dyed yellow.

HACKLED SPENT
Tail   Three or more fibres from the rump feather of a golden pheasant.
Body   Fluorescent white floss.
Rear hackle   Black cock.
Shoulder hackle   White, grizzle badger cock.

Tying a hawthorn fly

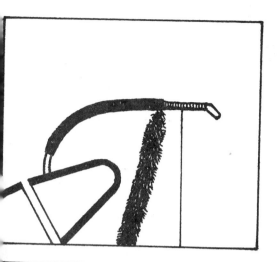

Place a size 10 or 12 down-eyed sproat hook in the vice and run tying silk from the eye to well around the bend. Tie in a length of black floss and take the silk and floss back two-thirds of the way along the shank. At this point, tie in a length of black chenille.

Just forward of the chenille, tie in two white cock hackle points.

Take the silk forward a little and wind the chenille carefully forward, around the wings, to build up a thorax.

Select a very long-fibred cock or hen hackle and tie in immediately forward of the thorax. Pull all the fibres down and trap the bases with tying silk, building up a head in the process. Whip finish and coat the head with black varnish.

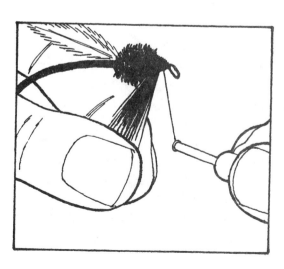

Tying a winged wet fly

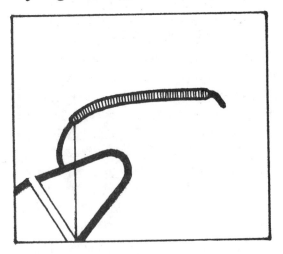

Clamp a down-eyed sproat hook in the vice and run a layer of waxed tying silk along the shank.

The characteristic bend of a sproat hook can be used to good effect by taking the tying silk well into the bend, giving the body a more natural, less rigid appearance

Select the tail material and tie it down with two or three turns of silk. Follow this with a length of ribbing, if required, and finally a length of body material. Return the tying silk back towards the eye leaving enough space to tie in the hackle and wings.

Wind the body material along the shank and tie it down. Follow this with the rib, which should be evenly spaced along the body.

I usually take a turn of ribbing around the hook shank before proceeding along the body.

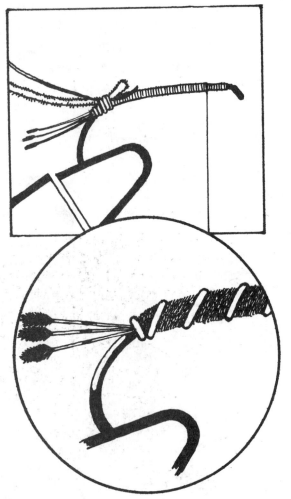

Trim off excess body and ribbing material in preparation for tying in the hackle and wings.

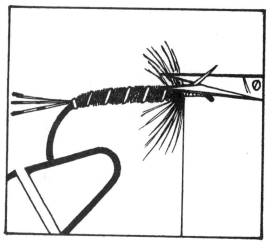

Select a hackle of the type required and tie down with the face of the feather looking forward, so that when it is wound on to the shank the fibres have a bias towards the bend of the hook. Two or three turns of hackle are ample. Tie down the hackle point and cut it away, then return the silk to the front of the hackle and trim off excess quill.

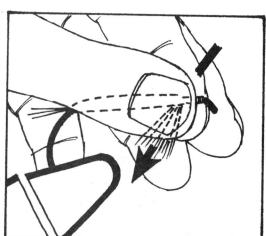

Moisten the forefinger and thumb and brush the hackle down and back. Make two or three turns of silk at the junction of the hackle and hook shank. The result should look like this.

Select two matching slips from a wing feather. Place them together so that the convex edges are facing outwards, opposite to those used on a dry fly.

Tying a winged wet fly (cont.)

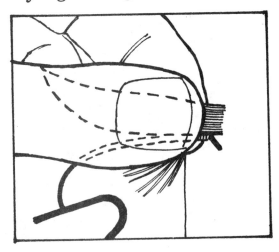

Grip the wing slips firmly between forefinger and thumb and position them on the hook shank. The point of the wings should just overlap the extreme end of the hook bend.

Clamp the wings firmly against the shank of the hook with two or three pinch and loops.

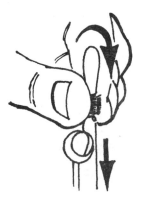

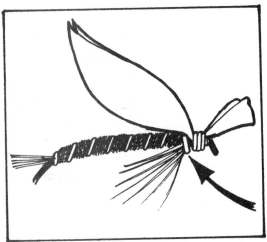

If the wings need to be lifted a little in order to improve the appearance of the fly a turn of tying silk can be taken to the rear.

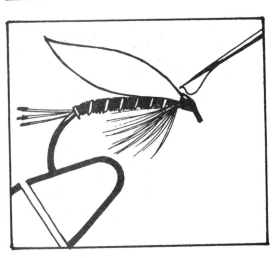

Trim away the excess wing material, build up a stream-lined head and whip finish.

Finally, using the dubbing needle, give the head a coat of varnish.

Winged wet fly dressings

SILVER MARCH BROWN
Tail   Fibres from partridge back feather.
Body   Flat silver tinsel, ribbed oval silver tinsel.
Hackle   Partridge back feather.
Wings   From hen pheasant wing.

ALEXANDRA
Tail   Red ibis feather slip.
Body   Flat silver tinsel.
Hackle   Black hen.
Wings   Six to eight strands of green peacock sword herl, with a slip of red ibis each side.

BUTCHER
Tail   Red ibis slip.
Body   Flat silver tinsel.
Hackle   Black hen.
Wings   From the blue wing-feather of a mallard drake.

ALDER
Body   Peacock herl ribbed with claret tying silk.
Hackle   Black hen.
Wings   From a brown speckled hen's wing feather.

PETER ROSS
Tail   Fibres from a golden pheasant tippet feather.
Body   Rear half — Flat silver tinsel. Front half — Dyed red seal's fur.
Rib   Oval silver tinsel over both halves.
Hackle   Black hen.
Wings   From the breast or flank feather of a teal.

MALLARD & CLARET
Tail   Fibres from a golden pheasant tippet feather.
Body   Claret seal's fur.
Rib   Oval gold tinsel.
Hackle   Natural red cock.
Wings   Bronze speckled feather from a mallard shoulder.

CONNEMARA BLACK
Tail Golden pheasant crest feather.
Body Black seal's fur, ribbed with fine oval tinsel.
Hackle Natural black cock beneath blue jay fibres.
Wings From the bronze shoulder feather of a mallard.

PARMACHENE BELLE
Tail Red and white duck feather.
Butt Black ostrich herl.
Body Yellow floss silk, ribbed with flat gold tinsel.
Hackle Dyed scarlet cock and white cock.
Wings White duck with a red ibis slip each side.

DUNKELD
Tail Golden pheasant crest.
Body Flat gold tinsel, ribbed with oval gold tinsel.
Hackle Dyed orange cock tied palmer fashion.
Wings Bronze mallard.
Cheeks Two jungle cock feathers.

PROFESSOR
Tail Red ibis feather slip.
Body Yellow floss silk, ribbed with gold tinsel.
Hackle Natural ginger cock.
Wing From the flank feather of a grey mallard.

INVICTA
Tail Golden pheasant crest feather.
Body Yellow seal's fur, ribbed with oval gold tinsel.
Body hackle Ginger cock.
Head hackle Blue jay fibres.
Wings From a hen pheasant tail feather.

ROYAL COACHMAN
Tail Strands from a golden pheasant tippet.
Body Scarlet floss with a bronze peacock herl butt and thorax.
Hackle Natural light red cock.
Wings Slips from any white wing feather.

Tying a corixa (water-boatman)

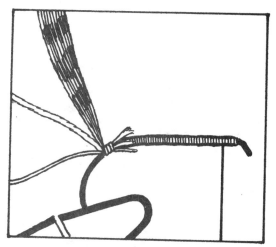

Clamp a size 12-14 down-eyed hook in the vice and run tying silk to the bend. Tie in a length of wire or oval tinsel ribbing, followed by a length of green or orange wool. Take a slip of fibres from a cock pheasant tail feather and tie at the same point, then run the silk back, almost to the eye.

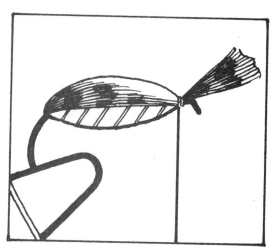

Build up a body with the wool and tie it down. Run the ribbing in neat spirals back along the body and tie it down. Trim off excess body and rib material.

Now pull the pheasant fibres right over the body, tie down and trim away excess material.

Select two long fibres from a cock pheasant tail and tie on at each side of the head. The thicker ends of the fibres should point to the rear. Build up a large head and treat it with a coat of clear varnish. A layer of clear varnish over the back is also advisable.

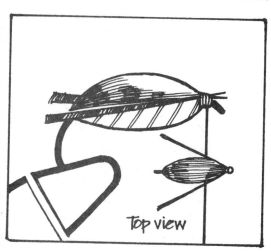

Top view

Tying a hackled wet fly

Hackles used for this type of fly need to be soft. Partridge, hen, snipe or woodcock are ideal.

When fished in running water the fibres of these hackles move in the current, giving the fly a most life-like appearance.

Place a down-eyed size 14-10 hook in the vice and tie in a body.

Select a good quality hackle and tether it to the hook shank with the face of the feather pointing forwards. Hold the tip of the hackle with hackle pliers and make just two or three turns around the shank.

Trim off excess hackle tip and quill, build up a neat head and coat it with clear varnish.

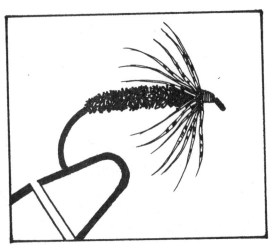

Hackle before preparation

Hackle ready to be tied

Hackled wet fly dressings

PARTRIDGE & ORANGE
Body   Bright orange floss or silk.
Hackle Brown partridge back feather.

BROWN SPIDER
Body   Bronze peacock herl.
Hackle Brown partridge back feather.

SNIPE & PURPLE
Body   Purple floss.
Hackle Small feather from snipe's wing.

BRACKEN CLOCK
Body   Bronze peacock herl and red silk.
Hackle Cock pheasant neck feather.

BLACK SPIDER
Body   Black tying silk or floss.
Hackle Black hen hackle.

WATERHEN BLOA
Body   Mole fur spun on yellow silk.
Hackle Feather from underside of moorhen's wing.

BLACK & PEACOCK SPIDER
Body   Three strands of peacock herl over black floss underbody.
Hackle Black hen hackle.

GROUSE & YELLOW
Body   Yellow floss silk ribbed with fine gold wire.
Hackle Grouse breast feather.

Tying a palmer

Run the tying silk from the eye to the bend of the hook and tie in a length of wire or tinsel. Tie in a length of body material and wind the silk back to a position just short of the eye. Wind the body material to this point, tie down and trim away any excess. Prepare and tie in a hackle against the front of the body.

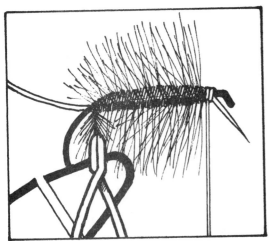

Grip the hackle point in a pair of hackle pliers and take the hackle, around the body, to the bend of the hook. Now, very carefully but firmly, wind the ribbing back through the hackle and tie it down with the silk. The ribbing is now holding the hackle stem secure all along the body.

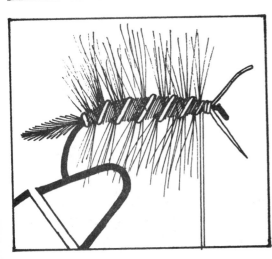

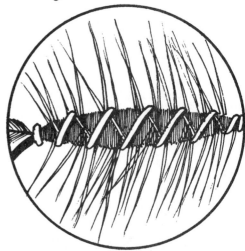

Remove the hackle pliers and trim away the hackle point, excess quill and ribbing material.

An extra hackle can now be tied at the front, if required. In my opinion this improves the appearance of the fly and helps to provide extra buoyancy if it is being used as a floating pattern.

On predominantly dark patterns a white forward hackle aids visibility when the fly is being fished in shadow beneath overhanging foliage.

Palmer dressings

BROWN PALMER
Body   Brown wool or seal's fur.
Rib   Gold wire or oval gold tinsel.
Hackle Brown cock.

STEEL BLUE
Body   Peacock herl with orange tag.
Rib   Gold wire.
Hackle Grizzle cock.

ZULU
Tail   Red ibis feather or red wool.
Body   Black wool or seal's fur.
Rib   Flat silver tinsel.
Hackle Black cock.

ARTFUL DODGER
Body   Purple wool.
Rib   Gold wire.
Wings From a cock pheasant's wing.
Hackle Red cock.

Tying a nymph

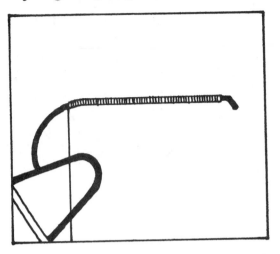

Place a long-shanked hook in the vice and run tying silk from the eye to the bend.

Tie in the tail material, if needed, followed by the ribbing and the body material.

In this instance we will assume that the body is made of seal's fur, which has to be dubbed on to the tying silk prior to being wound along the hook shank. (see section on dubbing a body).

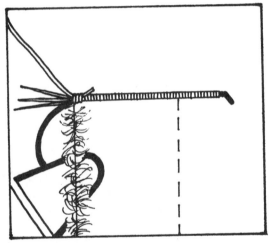

Take the dubbed silk, in turns, about two-thirds of the way back along the hook shank. Remove any excess dubbing from the hanging silk. Now carefully wind the rib material along the body and tie it down. A slip of feather fibres is now tied in by one end, which eventually forms the wing cases.

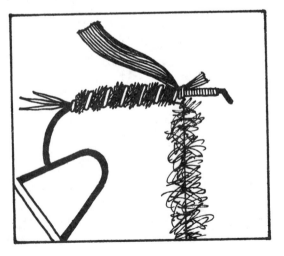

More seal's fur is now dubbed on to the silk in preparation for forming the thorax. This is usually a different colour to the main body. Remember not to overdo the dubbing as this will result in a bulky mess.

Wind the dubbed silk towards the eye of the hook. Stop just short of the eye, leaving enough space to tie in the hackle and form the head.

The hackle is tied in exactly the same way as that of a hackled wet fly. Trim away any excess hackle quill.

Now grip the end of the feather fibres and pull them over the thorax and the hackle. Tie down with a few turns of silk and trim away any excess material. Build a neat head, whip finish, trim off silk and varnish.

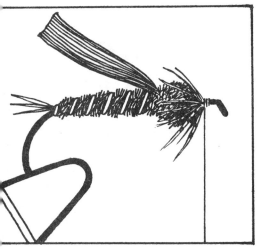

Some patterns of nymph have wing cases over the body or over the body and thorax.

Wing cases tied in at the bend of the hook and pulled over before the thorax is dubbed.

Wing cases tied in at the bend of the hook and pulled over before the head is formed.

Nymph dressings

SEDGE PUPA (JOHN GODDARD)

Body	Orange seal's fur.
Rib	Oval silver tinsel.
Thorax	Dark brown condor herl.
Wing cases	Pale brown condor herl.
Hackle	Honey hen, tied sparsely.

MAYFLY NYMPH

Tail	Three strands from a cock pheasant's tail feather.
Body	Natural seal's fur.
Thorax	Brown olive seal's fur.
Rib	Oval gold tinsel.
Wing cases	From a hen pheasant tail.
Hackle	Brown partridge.

AMBER NYMPH

Body	Amber yellow seal's fur.
Thorax	Dark brown or orange seal's fur.
Wing cases	Fibres of any brownish feather tied over the body.
Hackle	Honey hen hackle fibres.

DAMSELFLY NYMPH

Tail	Three olive green hackle points.
Body	Olive seal's fur.
Rib	Flat gold tinsel.
Thorax	Dark olive seal's fur.
Wing cases	Fibres from a brown mallard shoulder feather.
Hackle	Grouse hackle fibres.

MONTANA STONE

Body	Black chenille.
Thorax	Yellow or orange chenille.
Wing cases	Black chenille.
Hackle	Black hen.

IVEN'S GREEN & BROWN NYMPH

Tail	Three strands of peacock herl.
Body	Olive green ostrich herl.
Wing cases	Peacock herl.
Thorax	Peacock herl.

Tying a midge pupa (buzzer)

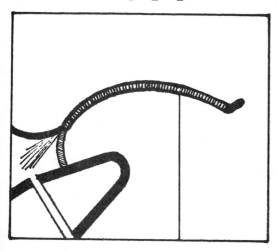

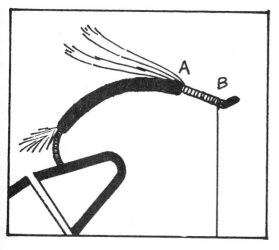

There are many variations on this imitation and, no doubt, they all take their share of trout if fished correctly. My variation is no exception and is simplicity itself to tie.

Place a size 16–10 Yorkshire caddis hook in the vice and run well waxed tying silk from the eye to well around the bend. Tie in a plume made from a short length of fluorescent white floss. A tap with the finger on the end of the floss will open it out.

Tie in a length of brown, black or green floss and take the tying silk back to point A. Wind on the floss body and tie down.

Tie in two or three lengths of fluorescent white floss and wind the silk to point B. Wind the strands of white floss, together, to point B, and tie down. Whip finish and varnish.

The plume at the front may have to be trimmed, and a few taps with the finger will open out the fibres to give a natural appearance.

189

Tying a lure (hackle-winged)

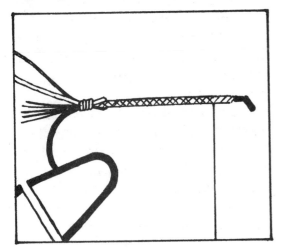

Clamp a down-eyed long-shanked hook in the vice and run well-waxed silk, in open turns, up to the bend. Tie in the tail, if needed, followed by the ribbing and the body material and run the silk back just short of the eye.

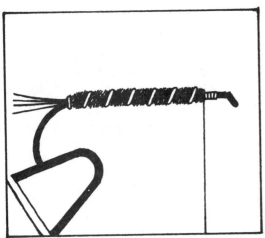

Wind the body material back to the hanging silk and tie it down. Do the same with the rib, making sure that it is evenly spaced all the way along the body. Trim off excess material.

Select two long, good quality cock hackles and hold them, back-to-back, between forefinger and thumb along the top of the body. The hackle points should extend just beyond the bend of the hook. Using the pinch and loop method, tie them down with three or four turns of silk.

Owing to their scarcity and price jungle cock feathers are not used as often as they once were. However, there are signs that they will once again be readily available in the not-too-distant future, as the bird is being reared in captivity by a few enterprising and imaginative breeders. If you do possess any of these striking feathers now is the point at which to tie them in, on each side of the wings. Check to see that they are positioned nicely before proceeding any further.

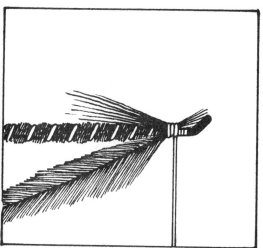

Turn the hook over in the vice. Pull off a bunch of fibres from a cock hackle, and using the pinch and loop method secure them with two or three turns of silk. Before tying them down completely, rub across the fibres with the thumb nail to spread them a little.

Build up a sleek-looking head and whip finish. Coat the head with red or black varnish. An eye decoration can be painted on if jungle cock is not being used.

Tying a lure (hair-winged)

Place a long-shanked down-eyed hook in the vice and run well-waxed tying silk down to the bend. Using the required materials, make the body in the usual manner.

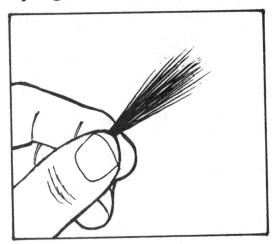

Cut a bunch of hairs of the required variety and lay it along the top of the hook shank. The tips of the hairs should extend just beyond the bend of the hook.

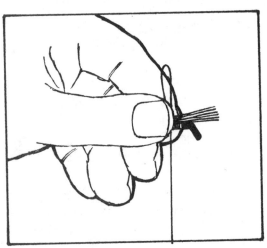

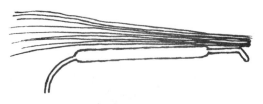

Take three or four turns of silk around the hairs and hook-shank using the pinch-and-loop procedure.

Half hitch

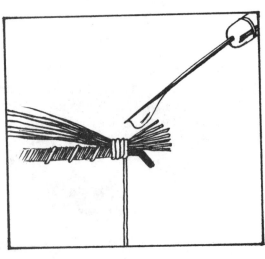

To prevent the fibres coming adrift during use, apply a blob of clear varnish which will be sucked into the wing by the capillary action of the hairs. Take a few more turns of silk around the hairs and make a half hitch.

Turn the fly over in the vice and tie on a beard hackle in exactly the same way as for the hackle-winged lure, and trim off any excess hackle.

Turn the fly upright again and trim off any excess wing material.

When trimming off excess wing material, cut at an angle, in order to produce a neater head.

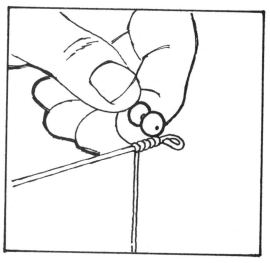

An additional embellishment for hackle or hairwing lures can be made by cutting a section of ball chain and tying this, in the manner shown, to produce a bug-eyed look.

Dressing omitted for the sake of clarity.

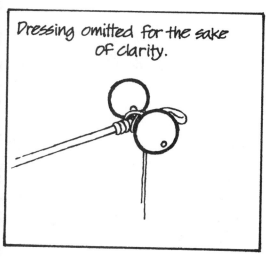

Lure dressings

MISSIONARY
Tail   Scarlet-dyed cock hackle
        Fibres.
Body   White chenille.
Rib   Silver tinsel.
Wing   Whole mallard breast Feather.
Hackle Scarlet-dyed cock hackle
        Fibres.

JERSEY HERD
Tail and Back Fibres of bronze
               peacock herl.
Body   Shaped with silk and covered
        with gold tinsel.
Hackle Hot orange cock.
Head   Two or three turns of
        peacock herl.

BADGER LURE
Body   Fluorescent orange wool.
Rib   Oval silver tinsel.
Wing   Two large badger cock hackles.
Hackle Hot orange cock hackle Fibres.
Eyes   Two jungle cock Feathers.

VIVA
Tag   Lime green fluorescent wool.
Body   Black chenille.
Rib   Flat silver tinsel.
Wing   Black marabou fibres.
Hackle Black cock hackle fibres.

ACE OF SPADES
Body   Black chenille.
Rib   Oval silver tinsel.
Wing   Black hen hackle tied
        matuka Fashion.
Overwing Bronze mallard.
Hackle Guinea fowl fibres.

RED & BLACK MATUKA
Body   Red chenille.
Rib   Oval gold tinsel.
Wing   Two black hen hackles tied
        matuka Fashion.
Eyes   Jungle cock Feathers.
Hackle Black cock hackle fibres.

SWEENEY TODD
Body   Rear— Black floss silk.
        Front— DFM magenta floss.
Rib   Silver tinsel or Lurex.
Hackle Crimson cock.
Wing   Black squirrel tail hair.

JACK FROST
Tag   Crimson wool.
Body   White wool.
Hackles Crimson cock followed by
         white cock.
Wing   White marabou.

CHURCH FRY
Tail   Bunch of white hackle fibres.
Body   Orange chenille.
Rib   Gold or silver tinsel.
Hackle Crimson.
Wing   Natural grey squirrel tail hair.

BLACK LURE
(Often tied tandem fashion)
Body   Black chenille or floss.
Rib   Silver tinsel.
Hackle Black cock fibres.
Wing   Four black cock hackles.

WHISKY FLY
Silk   Orange
Tag   DFM scarlet nylon floss.
Body   Wide silver tinsel or Lurex.
Rib   DFM scarlet nylon floss.
Hackle Hot orange cock.
Wing   Hot orange calf's tail hair.

BLACK GHOST
Tail   Golden pheasant crest.
Body   Black wool or floss.
Rib   Flat silver tinsel.
Hackle Golden pheasant crest.
Wing   White cock hackles.
Cheeks Jungle cock.

Tying a tandem lure

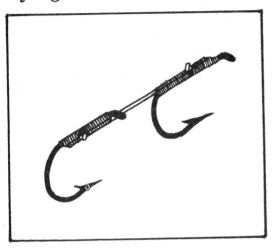

Tandem lures can be tied on long-shank or standard hooks. Cut a length of heavy nylon monofilament line and whip it to two hooks with heavy tying silk. Form a couple of simple hitch knots on the nylon line to prevent it slipping under the whipping. Reinforce this with a coat of clear varnish and allow to dry.

The example shown here is a worm fly, a long-established lure with many large trout to its credit.

Put the rear hook in the vice first and run the tying silk to the bend of the hook. Tie in a tail of red wool and a few fibres of peacock herl. Take the tying silk back, almost to the eye, and wind the body material to the same point and tie it down with silk.

Trim off any excess body herl and tie in a natural dark red hen or cock hackle to slope well back over the body. Whip finish and coat the head with black varnish.

The front hook is then put in the vice and tied in exactly the same manner as the rear hook. The tail, however, is omitted.

Long-shank hook tandem lures have only the body material tied to the rear hook.

Tandem lure dressings

BADGER LURE
Silk	Orange.
Bodies	Fluorescent orange wool.
Rib	Oval silver tinsel.
Hackle	Hot orange cock.
Wing	Two large badger hackles.
Eyes	Two jungle cock feathers.

BLACK LURE
Silk	Black.
Bodies	Black floss or chenille.
Rib	Oval silver tinsel.
Hackle	Black cock fibres.
Wing	Two or four long, black cock hackles.

SWEENEY TODD TANDEM
Silk	Black.
Bodies	Black floss silk.
Rib	Oval silver tinsel.
Throat	Magenta fluorescent wool.
Hackle	Crimson cock hackle fibres.
Wing	Black squirrel tail fibres.

CHURCH FRY TANDEM
Silk	Brown.
Bodies	Orange floss silk.
Rib	Flat silver tinsel or Lurex.
Throat	Magenta fluorescent wool.
Hackle	Orange cock hackle fibres.
Wing	Grey squirrel tail fibres.

Tying a muddler minnow

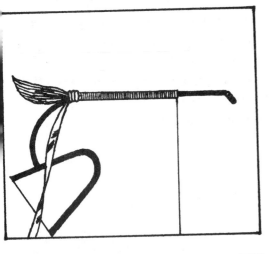

Wind black or brown tying silk from a point half way along the shank of a long-shanked hook to the bend. Tie in a slip of turkey wing for the tail and a length of flat gold tinsel, then return the silk to its starting point. Wind the gold tinsel to form a body, and tie it down.

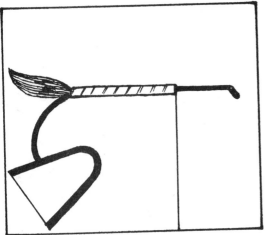

A bunch of grey squirrel tail hair is then tied to the shank to extend well beyond the bend of the hook.

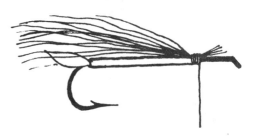

Two sections of mottled (oak) turkey feather are then tied over the squirrel hair, again extending past the bend of the hook. Make a half-hitch at this point in preparation for spinning the deer hair along the bare hook shank.

Cut a bunch of deer hair and grip it tightly to prevent the hairs sliding out of place.

Hold the hairs along the top of the hook shank with the cut ends pointing forward.

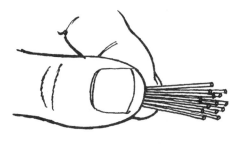

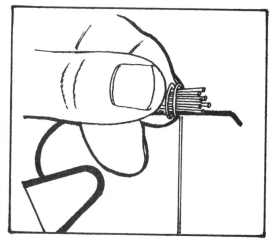

Take two loose turns of silk over the hairs.

Pull down tight on the silk, and at the same time rotate the finger and thumb in the same direction as the turning deer hair. The first spinning should look like this.

Take the silk to the front of the hairs and form a hitch, in readiness for the next spinning.

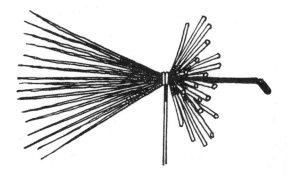

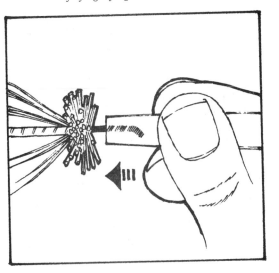

After each spinning the hairs will have to be pushed back. This is best done with an empty ball pen casing or something similar.

After a few spinnings the head will begin to take on a very bushy appearance. Hairs on the forward part of the head need not be full length as the head will have to be trimmed eventually. The drawing below shows how to obtain two spinnings from one length of hairs.

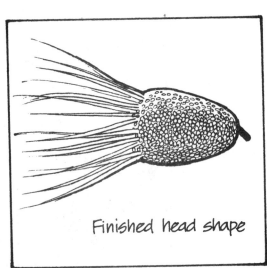

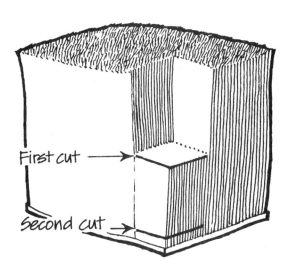

Spin the deer hair up to the eye, whip finish and varnish.

Very carefully start to trim the deer hair using sharp fly-tying scissors. The hair points forming the first spinning can be left to slope back over the body.

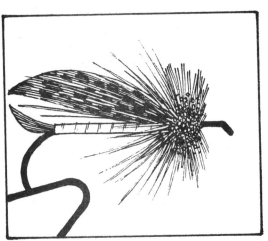

Finished head shape

Tying a jersey herd

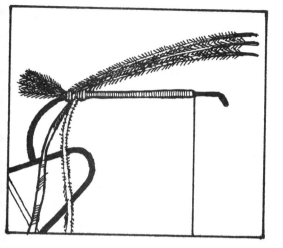

Place a long-shank No. 6-10 hook in the vice and run the tying silk down to the bend. Tie in a length of wool, flat gold tinsel and a bunch of peacock herl.

Take the silk back to a point short of the eye. Wind the wool towards the hanging silk, building up a cigar-shaped body in the process. Tie down the wool and trim off any excess. The gold tinsel is now wound over the wool body, tied down and trimmed.

Select a hot orange cock hackle and wind on in front of the body.

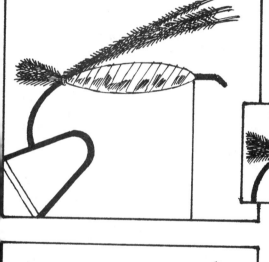

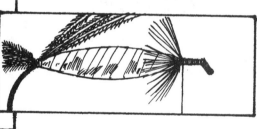

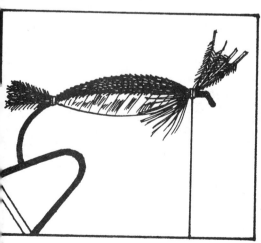

Bring the peacock herls over the body and hackle and tie them down, but do not trim away the excess herl.

Take the tying silk close to the eye and wind the excess herl around the shank to form a head.

Finish off in the usual manner.

Tying a matuka lure

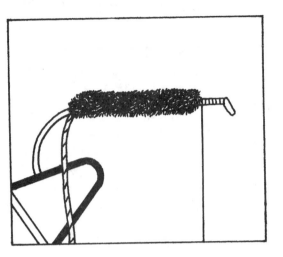

Place a long-shanked № 6–10 hook in the vice. Build up a body, which in most matuka patterns is made of chenille, and leave the rib (oval tinsel) hanging, ready for use.

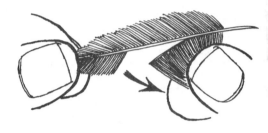

Select a large hen hackle and pull most of the fibres off on one side of the quill.

Place the prepared hackle on top of the body to see if it fits — the hackle should extend over the hook bend by about one-third of the body length. Take two or three turns of silk around the base of the quill to trap the hackle in position.

Very carefully start to wind the rib back through the hackle, adjusting the hackle fibres in the process. Tie down the rib, turn the fly over and tie in a beard hackle. Build up a head with the tying silk, whip finish and coat with black varnish.

Tying a dog nobbler

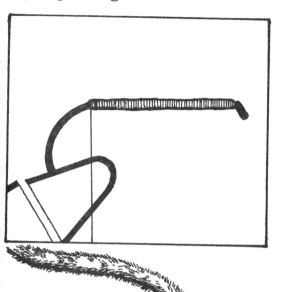

Put a long-shanked hook in the vice and take the tying silk to the bend of the hook.

Select a generous bunch of fibres from a marabou plume and tie in. Cut a length of chenille, tie it down next to the marabou and run the silk back to a point about 5mm short of the eye.

Wind the chenille along the hook shank to form a body, and tie down. Trim off any excess chenille and form a whip finish.

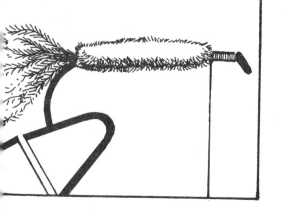

Smear a layer of waterproof glue over the shank of the hook between the body and the eye and squeeze on a non-toxic split shot. Final tightening with a gentle squeeze from a pair of pliers will guarantee a firm hold. Finally, give the shot a coat of black varnish.

Tying a shrimp

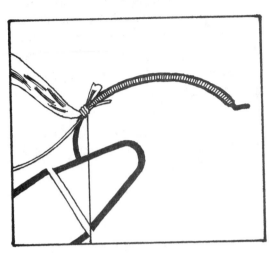

A curved-shank hook will be required to tie this very effective imitation. The 'caddis' hooks made by Partridge are ideal in sizes 16–10.

Take the silk from the eye to a point well around the bend and tie in a length of oval gold tinsel and a length of raffine or clear polythene.

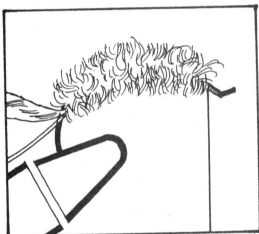

Wax the hanging tying silk and dub with seal's fur. Use a mixture of 90% cream or pale orange and 10% fluorescent red. Wind the dubbed silk to a point just short of the eye.

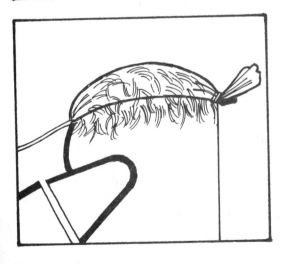

Pull the raffine or polythene completely over the top of the body, and tie it down.
If raffine is being used it must be dampened before doing this.

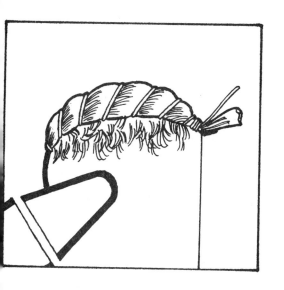

Now bring the ribbing, in neat spirals, over and along the body, and tie it down. Trim off the excess body shell material and ribbing and build up a neat head. Whip finish, and apply a coat of clear varnish over the head and shell back.

Tying silk colours for this pattern can be cream, orange, yellow or red.

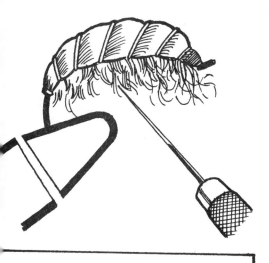

Using a dubbing needle, tease out strands of the body material to give a more life-like appearance.

This pattern can be tied to a standard-shank sproat hook, but in so doing ensure that the curved body shape is retained, by taking the dressing well around the hook bend.

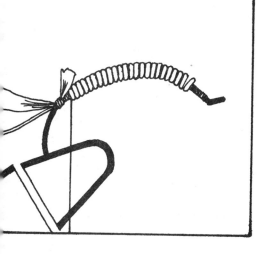

As this little creation is best fished well down in the water it is a good policy to add weight by running a length of lead wire along the shank of the hook before winding on the body.

Tying a daddy-long-legs

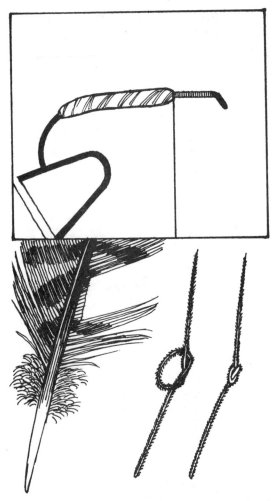

Clamp a long-shanked size 10 hook in the vice and run well-waxed tying silk from the eye to the bend. Tie in a length of raffia or raffine and bring the silk back about two-thirds of the way along the shank. Follow this with the body material, tie down and trim away any excess.

Cut a slip of fibres from a cock pheasant tail feather (the longer the better) and, one by one, separate them and tie a simple knot in the middle. Put these aside on a sheet of white paper or foam.

Turn the hook over in the vice. Select at least six fibres, more if you like, and hold them together between finger and thumb. Rotate them a few times to give a bedraggled look and tie them immediately in front of the body.

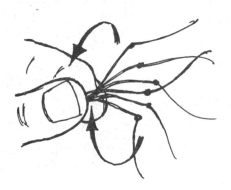

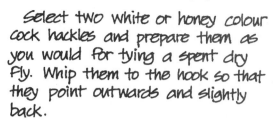

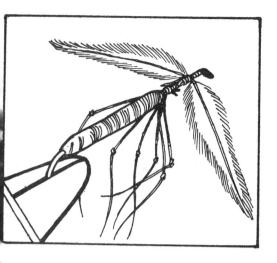

Select two white or honey colour cock hackles and prepare them as you would for tying a spent dry fly. Whip them to the hook so that they point outwards and slightly back.

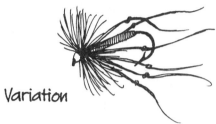

Variation

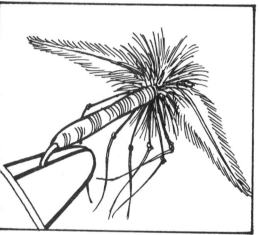

The hackle is then tied, using a natural red cock hackle, in exactly the same way as the hackle on a spent dry fly. Form a whip finish and coat the head with clear varnish.

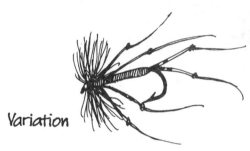

Variation

Tying a sedge (caddis) fly

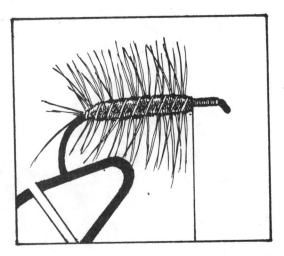

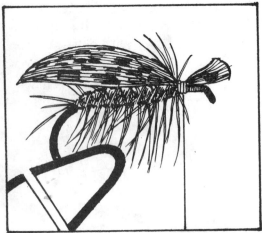

This is another pattern with many variations. Species of the natural insect are numerous and vary in size from the huge great red sedge or murragh, to the smaller sedges, such as silverhorns and yellow sedge.

A good impressionistic pattern can be made by tying a palmered body, as described earlier.

After the body is complete lay a matching pair of wing slips, taken from a mottled turkey tail feather or a hen pheasant wing feather, over the hackle, and tie down to lie low along the body. Immediately in front of the wings, tie in a good quality cock hackle.

This type of dressing provides enough buoyancy, when treated with floatant, to be dragged across the water surface, giving a life-like, scuttling impression of the natural insect.